10-6-76

How to
Get the Most
Out of Your
Low-Cost
Electronic Calculator

RONALD BENREY

HAYDEN BOOK COMPANY, INC.
Rochelle Park, New Jersey

Library of Congress Cataloging in Publication Data

Benrey, Ronald.
    How to get the most out of your low-cost electronic
calculator.

    1. Calculating-machines--Problems, exercises, etc.
I. Title.
QA75.B36   510'.28   76-4548
ISBN 0-8104-5942-6

1	2	3	4	5	6	7	8	9	PRINTING
76	77	78	79	80	81	82	83	84	YEAR

Preface

The electronic calculator is a revolutionary product in two ways: First, it represents a revolutionary transplanting of space-age electronic technology into our homes. And second, it provides us with a revolutionary capability for performing arithmetic and mathematical computations.

Unhappily, the majority of calculator owners never use the talents of their hand-held computers to the fullest. They are content to do little more than calculate their income tax refund once each year, and total up their checks at the end of each month. This is a pity, because even the least expensive "four-function" calculator is capable of doing much, much more.

Much, much more is what this book is all about! In the pages that follow, you will find scores of practical calculations—financial calculations, household calculations, hobby calculations, fun calculations, metric system calculations, area and volume calculations, and many others. The *algorithm* (or detailed procedure) for each calculation is presented in easy-to-understand *flow chart* format. Each algorithm is accompanied by a brief introduction that describes the procedure, and by a complete numerical example that illustrates the calculation. When necessary, separate algorithms are presented for each of the two common calculator keyboard configurations (some machines have a single "=" key; others have dual "+=" and "−=" keys).

The book also contains several conversion tables, reference charts, and equivalency tables that you will find both unusual and useful. In fact, I hope that this volume proves to be one of the handiest reference books in your personal library.

The introductory section that precedes the collection of algorithms is a "short course" on your calculator's innards and operating characteristics. I've included this material as a supplement to the instruction manual that came with your machine. Much of the information presented here will help you use your calculator more efficiently.

One final point: To use your calculator to best advantage, you must rethink the way you work with numbers. Until low-cost calculators came along, we all "guestimated"—rather than calculated—everyday quantities. It was simply too much work to compute the efficiency of home insulation, or figure the true interest on installment loans, or compare the energy consumption of two different air conditioners. Now that you own a calculator, "crunching numbers together" is easy, and almost fun. And so, I encourage you to search out practical uses for your palm-sized electronic brain. You will find that it will earn its keep many times over.

RONALD M. BENREY

Upper St. Clair, Pennsylvania

Contents

1
Introduction

Your new electronic calculator is probably the most sophisticated electronic device you have ever purchased (Fig. 1-1). Though it may be scarcely larger than a paperback novel (many models are barely bigger than packs of cigarettes), its electronic circuitry is far more complex than the innards of a TV set, or stereo receiver, or tape recorder. In fact, the heart of your calculator—the electronics that performs the arithmetic operations—is a circuit composed of *many thousands* of transistors and other components.

Cramming all of these electronic parts into such a small package was accomplished by an amazing process called *large-scale integration*, or LSI, for short (see Fig. 1-2). Specifically, the computing "wizard" inside your calculator is a *large-scale integrated circuit.*

LSI technology starts with a thin chip of silicon not much larger than a letter "O." Through an elaborate series of photographic and chemical processes, the complex circuit is created on and within the tiny chip. The various circuit components are built up of alternating layers of silicon material, silicon oxide, and metal film; the components are finally interconnected by a network of metal-film connections.

Viewed under a microscope, the finished circuit chip looks like an exquisitely-detailed inlaid floor since its thousands of circuit components are grouped in neat geometric patterns. The degree of miniaturization is staggering: the LSI circuit is equivalent to several chassisfuls of conventional electronic parts. And the cost-savings made possible by the technique are almost unbelievable. Just a few years ago, *four-function* calculators (machines that add, subtract,

1

Figure 1-1 Typical electronic calculators

multiply, and divide) built of conventional components cost thousands of dollars.

The LSI chip is too small and too fragile to be used as is. Thus it is sealed within a protective epoxy plastic or ceramic module about the size of a large postage stamp. The module has a set of leads (typically numbering twenty-eight) that serve to connect the chip circuitry to the various external components (keyboard, display, power supply, etc.)

Incidentally, LSI calculator modules are produced by only a handful of semiconductor manufacturers. Consequently, all but a few calculator manufacturers buy the modules they use. This explains the great similarity among the many different brands of four-function machines.

Inside a Four-Function Calculator

Before we go on to talk about using your new calculator, let's take a closer—but brief—look inside.* The "architecture" of a

*This section may tell you more about your calculator than you really want to know. If so, feel free to flip to "Keys and Controls" on page 8.

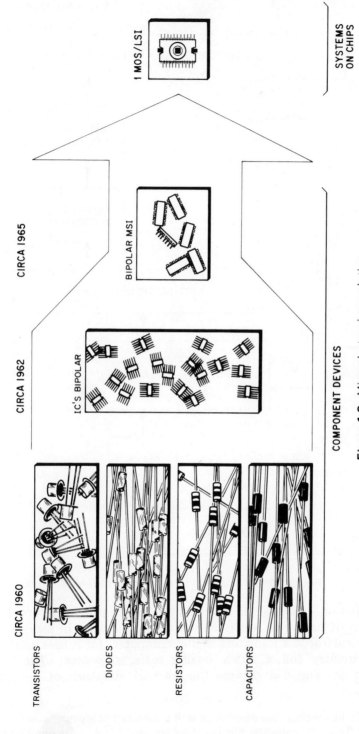

Figure 1-2 Microelectronics evolution

3

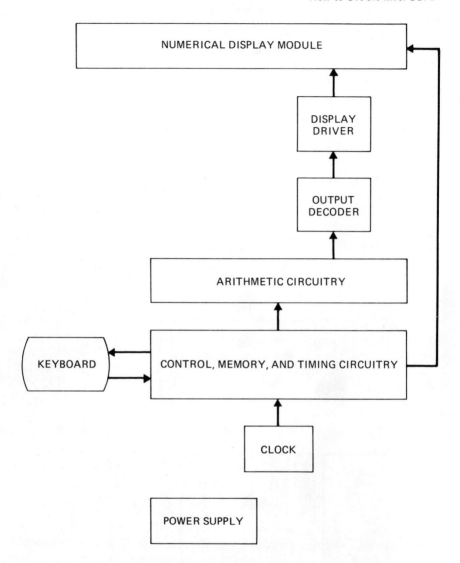

Figure 1-3   Internal structure of typical calculator

four-function calculator is fairly simple to understand if considered
in terms of its major functional "building blocks." In many ways,
your calculator is a miniature digital computer, for it uses much the
same circuitry (on a much smaller scale, of course). The block
diagram in Fig. 1-3 depicts the internal structure of a typical
machine.*

> *To be specific, this description is of a popular LSI module manufactured
> by Texas Instruments. Similar chips are used in calculators produced by
> several makers.

The *keyboard* has the most obvious function. You enter numbers and "commands" ("instructions" to add, multiply, subtract, or divide) by pressing its set of labeled push-button switches.

The *control, memory, and timing* circuitry block is the calculator's "brain." It is here that your keyed-in commands are interpreted and carried out, and it is here that the numbers you have entered are temporarily stored until they are needed in the computation. If your machine is equipped for "constant multiplication and division" (we'll talk about this feature later), the constant is stored in the memory circuits from where it can be repeatedly "recalled" as required. Similarly, if your calculator is equipped with a "memory register" that permits you to store and recall an answer or constant (more about this later, too), the necessary circuitry is part of this block.

Actually, there are two kinds of memory circuits within the LSI chip: the random-access memory (RAM) and the read-only memory (ROM).

Think of the RAM as an "electronic scratchpad"—a circuit that can remember numbers (that have been "translated" into corresponding electronic signals). Its name—random-access memory—reflects the fact that numbers can be *written* into any of the memory's storage cells (to store them) as required, and then *read out* (to recall them) when they are needed. This can be repeated as often as necessary, with new numbers replacing the previously stored numbers.

By contrast, the contents of the ROM were locked into it when the LSI chip was manufactured. Hence, it is a memory designed to be *read only*. The contents are never changed—in fact, it is physically impossible to change them. The ROM contains instructions (again, translated into electronic signals) rather than numbers. These instructions are available at the touch of a command key to direct specific operations. For example, when you touch the "X" key, the series of instructions needed to perform a multiplication is recalled from the ROM and fed to the control circuitry. In turn, the *arithmetic circuitry* is directed to multiply together the two numbers you have inputted via the keyboard.

The *timing circuitry* has the important job of synchronizing the many different chip functions. As you might expect, the internal movements of numbers and instructions must take place with the grace and precision of a ballet dance. The "dancing master" (so to speak) is a circuit located outside the LSI module that is called, logically enough, the *clock*. This circuit generates a steady stream of pulses (approximately 250,000 per second) that is the calculator's heart beat.

The *arithmetic circuit* performs the actual numerical computations. In common with all digital computer circuits, the arithmetic circuits works with digits that are expressed in the *binary number system*. Specifically, the ten familiar decimal digits (0 through 9) are expressed in *binary-coded decimal* form, using the two binary digits (0 and 1) as follows:

$$0 = 0000$$
$$1 = 0001$$
$$2 = 0010$$
$$3 = 0011$$
$$4 = 0100$$
$$5 = 0101$$
$$6 = 0110$$
$$7 = 0111$$
$$8 = 1000$$
$$9 = 1001$$

The great advantage of using the binary number system is that the calculating circuitry need deal only with two different digits— namely 0 and 1—instead of ten digits. Thus the circuitry can be built up of numerous "two state" switching circuits, wherein one voltage level represents a binary "0" and a second level represents binary "1." Even though it takes four binary digits to represent a single decimal digit, the inherent simplicity and reliability of two-state circuitry makes this "trade off" worthwhile.

Of course, you want to see decimal digit answers to your computations. Making this happen is the job of the *output decoder circuit*. It transforms the module's internal binary number representations into electronic signals that cause the *numerical display module* to display the corresponding decimal digits. The *display driver* (located between the decoder and the display module) boosts the decoder output signals to the level necessary to operate the display.

Several different types of *numerical displays* are used in calculators but virtually all have a common denominator: they are so-called "seven segment" displays. The display unit for each decimal digit consists of seven individual segments arranged in a figure-eight. By causing selected combinations of segments to glow, any decimal digit can be displayed (Fig. 1-4).

Most small calculators have eight-digit displays. This means that

Figure 1-4   Display of decimal digits.

the largest displayable number is 99999999, and the smallest is 0.0000001. "Desk-model" machines may have ten, twelve, or even sixteen-digit displays. Besides eight digits, the typical calculator display module has a dot-sized decimal point placed at the right side of each digit (a total of eight decimal points) that is controlled by the circuitry within the chip, and a few additional segments that form minus signs "–" and assorted E or ⊔ shapes to indicate that the arithmetic circuit is "overflowing" (the number being handled exceeds the circuit's capacity). If your calculator is equipped with a memory register, the display will be capable of indicating—via an unusual symbol—that a number is stored in memory.

Virtually all low-cost, four-function calculators use one of the following technologies for making the display segments glow (or, at least, be visible):

1. *Light-emitting diodes* (LED), in which the individual segments are composed of diode "junctions" (sometimes a single junction; occasionally two or three) that emit light when fed an electric current. Most LED displays glow bright red. Since the actual glowing region is a tiny pinpoint, many LED displays have plastic "light pipes" atop the diodes to spread the illumination over a segment length. Because LED displays draw a substantial amount of current, battery-powered calculators that use them are often equipped with a time delay circuit that automatically dims the display after a few seconds. You can restore the display by touching a special key, or (in some calculators) the "=" key.

2. *Planar gas-discharge displays*, which are cousins to the familiar neon lamps you see in store windows. The glow is produced by an electric current flowing through a thin layer of ionized gas (the gas inside is neon, with a bit of mercury vapor added). The glow is red-orange in color, but simple filters can be installed out front to produce an amber, orange, or red glow.

3. *Vacuum-fluorescent tube*, which operates much like a TV picture tube. Each of the seven segments is an individual "anode." Electrons emitted from the "cathode" strike the anodes, making them emit a cool, bluish-green light.

4. *Liquid-crystal display*, which doesn't emit light but merely reflects ambient room light. Voltages applied across the normally transparent "liquid crystal" material within the display cell cause selected segments to appear opaque, making the digit visible.

A particularly interesting aspect of calculator architecture that is not apparent in the block diagram is the *multiplexed operation* of the keyboard and display circuits. Essentially, multiplexing simplifies the wiring between the keyboard and display and the IC chip. This is a thorny problem to handle without multiplexing. Here's why: You'll observe that a typical eight-digit calculator display has 56 display segments for number display (7 segments × 8 digits = 56), plus eight decimal points, plus the additional segments for minus sign and overflow indication, a total of perhaps 70 individual elements that must be controlled by the LSI module. Similarly, the keyboard may have 20 different keys (including 10 digits, the decimal point key, mathematical operation keys, etc.).

Seventy display elements plus twenty keyboard switches means that 90 "things" must be connected—somehow—to the LSI module. Connecting each individually would require complex wiring and a massive IC package laden with terminals. The cost would be prohibitive!

Multiplexing does the job via a system of repeated scanning. Essentially, the LSI module rapidly scans across the keyboard switches (searching for input numbers and commands) and the display circuitry (sequentially delivering output pulses to the display segments). The process repeats several hundred times each second; each scan takes place so quickly that you cannot notice any time delay when you operate the keyboard, or any flicker when you view the display.

Finally, there is the power supply. Its job is to supply the necessary voltages and currents for the LSI module and external circuitry.

Keys and Controls

Virtually all four-function calculators can be grouped in one of two categories:

1. Calculators having a single equals key (simply labeled "=").
2. Calculators having two "dual function" equals keys (labeled "+=" and "−=").

Figure 1-5 illustrates the two variations (we show typical, rather than actual, keyboards). Broadly speaking, the dual equals key arrangement (Fig. 1-5A) tends to simplify the totaling up of long columns of numbers (say a list of debits and credits on a balance sheet); thus it is found on most "business" and/or "office" calculators. On the other hand, the single equals key configuration (Fig. 1-5B) simplifies "linked" computations, that is, calculations involving a series of assorted additions, subtractions, multiplications, and divisions done sequentially to come up with a final answer. Thus, the single equals key is found on most "technical" and/or "scientific" calculators.

It's impossible to say that one system is better than the other

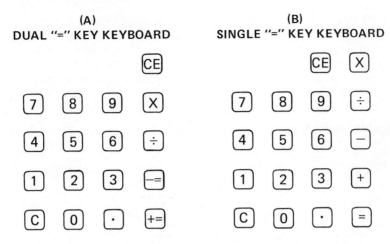

Figure 1-5 The two categories of four-function calculators

since both have advantages. The dual-key approach emulates a mechanical adding machine; the single-key system is more "logical" as you think your way through a series of computations. Because both keyboard configurations are in widespread use, and because they occasionally require different keying procedures for identical computations, the calculation algorithms throughout this book will sometimes include two procedures: the single equals key procedure first and the dual equals key procedure second (when procedures for both keyboards are identical, only a single example will be shown).*

Example 1-1 shows what we mean and illustrates a few of the operational differences between the two keyboard plans.

As you can see, the obvious procedural differences pretty much center upon how negative numbers (−7, for example) are manipulated. A more subtle difference is the fact that the single equals key acts as a "grand total" or "end of computation" key. The calculator automatically clears itself of all entered numbers and results (although the final answer remains displayed). Thus you can begin a new computation simply by entering a new number. This is not true of a dual equals key machine. You must manually clear the machine—by pressing the "C" key—before going on to a new *addition* or *subtraction* calculation, as shown in Example 1-2. Note that successive multiplication or division calculations *can* be done on a dual equals key machine without clearing between each computation, as shown in Example 1-3.

*As more and more calculators are produced, the trend seems to be towards the single-equals key configuration. This is apparently because this design is a bit less confusing to master.

Example 1-1: Total the following column of numbers:

$$+8$$
$$-7$$
$$+6$$
$$\overline{?}$$

Single "=" key keyboard   *Dual "=" key keyboard*

keyboard	display	keyboard	display
C	0.	C	0.
8	8.	8	8.
−	8.	+=	8.
7	7.	7	7.
+	1.	−=	1.
6	6.	6	6.
=	7.	+=	7.

Example 1-2: Total the following two columns of numbers on a dual "=" key calculator:

$$+6 \qquad +5$$
$$+4 \qquad +7$$
$$\overline{?} \qquad \overline{?}$$

Clearing between additions

keyboard	display	keyboard	display
C	0.	5	5.
6	6.	+=	5.
+=	6.	7	7.
4	4.	+=	12.
+=	10.		
C	0.		

without clearing between additions

keyboard	display	keyboard	display
C	0.	5	5.
6	6.	+═	15.
+═	6.	7	7.
4	4.	+═	22.
+═	10.		

Example 1-3: Perform the following pair of computations:

    (1) $3 \times 4 \times 5 = ?$ (2) $\dfrac{5}{8} \times 12 = ?$

Single "=" key keyboard or dual "=" key keyboard

keyboard	display	
C	0.	
3	3.	
X	3.	
4	4.	
X	12.	
5	5.	
═ or +═	60.	*Answer 1.*
5	5.	
÷	5.	
8	8.	
X	0.625	
1 2	12.	
═ or +═	7.5	*Answer 2.*

NOTE EXCEPTION: This procedure may not work on calculators equipped for "automatic constant" operation (see page 15). When using a machine of this type, it may be necessary to press the clear key between sets of operations.

Example 1-4: Perform the following computation:

$$\frac{\frac{17}{68} \times 14}{36} = ?$$

Single "=" key keyboard or dual "=" key keyboard

keyboard	display
C	0.
1 7	17.
÷	17.
6 8	68.
×	0.25
1 4	14.
÷	3.5
3 6	36.
= or +═	0.0972222

Here's an important point: In the examples given, we multiplied a series of numbers together *without* touching the equals key between pairs of numbers. This "linking" of operations can be done on most calculators. Essentially, touching one of the arithmetic command keys completes the preceding operation and simultaneously readies the calculator for a new operation. Examples 1-4 and 1-5 illustrate what we mean.

Practically speaking, very few—if any—day-to-day calculations involve negative numbers. However, many calculators are equipped with a special key to simplify the handling of negative numbers. This key changes the sign of the number being displayed. It may be labeled "NE" (for *negative entry*), or "+/−", or even "SIGN." This key permits you to perform a calculation such as 7 × −5 = −35, a calculation that is impossible to perform on a single "=" key calculator not equipped with a sign-change key *unless* the sequence of numbers is reversed (i.e., −5 × 7 = −35).* This is because there is no way to change the sign of the second number without causing the

Example 1-5: Perform the following computation:

$$\frac{4}{5} \times \frac{7}{8} \times \frac{12}{17} = ?$$

Single "=" key keyboard or dual "=" key keyboard

keyboard	display
C	0.
4	4.
÷	4.
5	5.
X	0.8
7	7.0
÷	5.6
8	8.
X	0.7
1 2	12.
÷	8.4
1 7	17.
= or +=	0.4941176

machine to complete the calculation prematurely. Note: With a dual-equals key calculator, you *can* produce the correct answer by multiplying +7 and +5 with the use of the "−=" key. This can be a tricky business, though, since you must remember to switch to the "−=" key whenever a negative factor is involved.

An increasing number of calculators are equipped with a percent function key (usually labeled "%"). This is a handy feature

*As with most positive statements about electronic calculators, there are exceptions to this rule. A few single-equals key machines allow the entering of negative numbers through the use of the "−" key. The sequence of keystrokes to multiply 7 by −5 would be: "7", "X", "−", "5", "=". If you own a single-equals key calculator, try this sequence and see what happens.

Example 1-6:   Express 4/24 as a percentage.

Single "=" key keyboard or dual "=" key keyboard

With percent key   *Without percent key*

keyboard	display	keyboard	display
C	0.	C	0.
4	4.	4	4.
÷	4.	÷	4.
2 4	24.	2 4	24.
%	16.66666	X	0.1666666
		1 0 0	100.
		= or +═	16.66666

that saves a few keystrokes. Essentially, pressing the "%" key is equivalent to completing a division and then multiplying by 100, as shown in Example 1-6.

Decimal Points: Floating and Fixed

A floating decimal point, as its name implies, "floats" to wherever it is supposed to be. Thus, if you were to multiply 7.89 by 6.47, the answer (as seen during floating point operation) would be 51.0483. (You would see the same answer if you set the calculator for four-place fixed-point operation, but we'll ignore this fact right now). Similarly, dividing 1.9 by 832 yields 0.0022836 (on an eight-digit calculator). In both examples, the calculator automatically placed the decimal point—and selected the number of decimal places displayed—for maximum possible precision of the answer. For these reasons, floating-point calculator operation is sometimes labeled "automatic decimal point placement."

There are times, though, when you may wish to control the position of the decimal point—in effect, to *fix* the point at a specific number of decimal places. An obvious fixed-point situation is when you are making money calculations and thus prefer the decimal point fixed at two places to simplify reading the answers. Consequently, many calculators are equipped with a switch that lets the user select between floating-point operation and one or two fixed decimal point positions (most often two and four decimal places). A few machines even provide full flexibility by permitting the operator to select any fixed-point position from zero to eight decimal places. A handful of calculators allow *only* two-decimal-place fixed-point operation (this is a severe limitation for many types of calculations). Still other calculators are equipped only for floating-point operation (including most low-cost "pocket-size" machines).

During fixed-point operation, *some* calculators so equipped will automatically "truncate" the answer to the decimal precision you have specified, rather than "round it off." Thus, a truncating type calculator set for two decimal places will multiply 7.89 by 6.47 and display the answer 51.04. It simply lopped off the last two digits of the complete answer (51.0483). Had you performed the calculation by hand, you would probably have rounded off the answer to 51.05. Neither answer is more "correct" than the other, but the rounded-off result is usually preferred.

This characteristic is a potential source of confusion (and seemingly incorrect answers!). If your machine provides fixed-point operation, check the manual to see if it rounds off or truncates answers to the specified precision.

Another fixed-point mixup can occur when computations yield answers smaller than the decimal point setting allows. For example, a calculator set for two-decimal-place fixed-point operation will divide 1.9 by 832 and display 0.00 as the answer rather than 0.0022836. Since the majority of day-to-day calculations involve larger numbers, you will rarely encounter this problem. However, remember to set your calculator for floating-point operation whenever you work with either (1) small numbers, or (2) combinations of small and large numbers that could yield numerically small results when multiplied or divided together. (*Note*: All of the numerical examples that follow this section have been performed on an eight-digit calculator set for floating-point operation.)

"Constant" Multiplication and Division

Many familiar calculations are repetitive in nature when performed on a four-function calculator. Two familiar illustrations would be computing the growth of your savings given a specific compound interest rate, and raising a given number to a power (we'll discuss both in the algorithm section that follows this introduction). Similarly, you may wish to perform the same basic computation again and again, using a specific factor as a constant, for example, when calculating the sales tax on a series of items. Here, the tax rate (say 5 percent, or 0.05) is constant in each calculation.

The "constant" operation feature incorporated in all but the least expensive calculators dramatically simplifies these kinds of computations. Chances are, though, that you will find this the most confusing talent of your little computer, primarily because of the strict "rules and regulations" you must follow to make it work. A further complication stems from the fact that many calculators do not have a switch that turns the constant feature on and off. Instead, they have "automatic constant operation," meaning, essentially, that the feature is always turned on! So-called automatic operation is less desirable than switched operation because a careless touch on the equals key at the wrong time can spoil the calculation (we'll see how this happens later). Moreover, automatic constant operation makes it impossible to "chain together" (perform sequentially) assorted additions and subtractions *after* a multiplication or division has been performed on a dual-equals key machine (this is not true of a single-equals key calculator).

The principle behind constant operation is simple: The calculator "remembers"—and uses again and again—one of the two factors of a multiplication or division. Specifically, it stores the *multiplicand*

Example 1-7: Compute the sales tax (tax rate = 0.05, or 5-percent) on each of the following purchase prices: $12.50; $150; $35; and $850.

Single "=" key keyboard or dual "=" key keyboard

keyboard	display	
CONSTANT "ON"	—	
$\boxed{C}$	0.	
$\boxed{0}$ $\boxed{.}$ $\boxed{0}$ $\boxed{5}$	0.05	
$\boxed{\times}$	0.05	
$\boxed{1}$ $\boxed{2}$ $\boxed{.}$ $\boxed{5}$	12.5	
$\boxed{=}$ or $\boxed{+=}$	0.625	*Answer 1*
$\boxed{1}$ $\boxed{5}$ $\boxed{0}$	150.	
$\boxed{=}$ or $\boxed{+=}$	7.5	*Answer 2*
$\boxed{3}$ $\boxed{5}$	35.	
$\boxed{=}$ or $\boxed{+=}$	1.75	*Answer 3*
$\boxed{8}$ $\boxed{5}$ $\boxed{0}$	850.	
$\boxed{=}$ or $\boxed{+=}$	42.5	*Answer 4*

Example 1-8:   Convert the following poundages to kilograms: 19; 480; 53; 22.4

Single "=" key or dual "=" key keyboard

keyboard	display	
CONSTANT "ON"	—	
C	0.	
1 9	19.	
÷	19.	
2 . 2 0 5	2.205	
= or +=	8.61678	*Answer 1*
4 8 0	480.	
= or +=	217.68707	*Answer 2*
5 3	53.	
= or +=	24.036281	*Answer 3*
2 2 4	22.4	
= or +=	10.15873	*Answer 4*

(first factor) for multiplication (multiplicand × multiplier = product) and the *divisor* (second factor) for division (dividend ÷ divisor = quotient).* Let's demonstrate with the sales tax problem mentioned earlier, as shown in Example 1-7. Here, the factor 0.05 is used again and again in the series of multiplications. Note that the calculator remembers the multiplication command (i.e., "×") also. Thus, each operation is performed simply by entering the new item price (the multiplier) and touching the "=" key (or "+=").

As another example, let's convert a series of weight values expressed in pounds into the metric system weight measure of kilograms. To make the conversions, each poundage value must be divided by 2.205, as shown in Example 1-8. To "break the chain"

---

*At least one manufacturer of calculators goes against this arrangement and produces machines that "remember" the *second* factor in both multiplication and division. Thus, division operations using a constant will be identical to Example 1-7, whereas multiplication operations require that the order of the factors be reversed.

and return to normal computation, either clear the calculator or begin a new computation.

Accidental use of the constant operation feature can ruin ordinary calculations. Example 1-9 illustrates two possibilities:

Example 1-9:   Perform the following pair of computations:

(1) $5 \times 7 = ?$ (2) $(2 \times 8) + 5 = ?$

Computation 1

Single "=" key keyboard or dual "=" key keyboard

keyboard		display
CONSTANT "ON"		—
C		0.
5		5.
X		5.
7		7.
= or +=		35.
= or +=	*Accidental Keystroke*	245.

Computation 2

Single "=" key keyboard—procedure yields the correct answer

keyboard	display
CONSTANT "ON"	—
C	0.
2	2.
X	2.
8	8.
+	16.
5	5.
=	21.

Dual "=" key keyboard—procedure yields the wrong answer

keyboard	display	
CONSTANT "ON"	—	
$\boxed{\text{C}}$	0.	
$\boxed{2}$	2.	
$\boxed{\times}$	2.	
$\boxed{8}$	8.	
$\boxed{+=}$	16.	
$\boxed{5}$	5.	
$\boxed{+=}$	10.	*Wrong Answer*

1. An accidental extra keystroke (on the "=" or "+=" key) when the calculator is in the constant operation mode

2. Attempting to link together addition (or subtraction) operations and multiplication (or division) operations on a dual-equals key calculator.

The point is this: Constant operation is a handy capability, but learn its limitations and requirements.

Using Your Memory

An independent *memory register* was once the hallmark of a high-priced desk-top calculator. Now this very useful feature is filtering down to inexpensive, pocket-sized machines. Essentially, the memory is a "place" to temporarily store a number during a long calculation (one involving a series of different computations). The stored number may be a constant used several times during the calculations (say the cost of a square yard of carpeting, when the total cost of carpeting a home is being computed), or it may be an "intermediate result" (the result of an earlier calculation that will be used in a later step). Occasionally, the stored number is an "accumulation"—or sum—of several intermediate results.

A good example of the last possibility is the process of totaling up the square footage of wall space in your living room before ordering wall paper or paint. Here, the final answer—that is, the total wall area—is the accumulation of four separate wall areas minus the areas of windows and doors. Most calculator memories are controlled by "M+" and "M−" keys,* a duo that makes this kind of calculation easy. Specifically, the "M+" key adds the current answer (or entry) to the number already stored in memory, and the new answer then

*A few machines equipped with memory have a single "M" key that is used in conjunction with the "+" and "−" keys. Thus, to initiate an "M+" operation, the user presses the "M" and "+" keys in sequence.

Example 1-10: Find the area to be painted in a room that measures 12 feet by 16 feet and has a ceiling height of 8 feet. The door and window area is 30 square feet.

Single "=" key keyboard or dual "=" key keyboard

keyboard		display
CONSTANT "ON"		−
C *		0.
8		8.
X		8.
1 2		12.
= or +═		96.
M+		96.
M+		96.
MR	*OPTIONAL KEYSTROKE*	192.
1 6		16.
= or +═		128.
M+		128.
M+		128.
MR	*OPTIONAL KEYSTROKE*	448.
3 0		30.
M−		30.
MR		418.

*If the calculator memory has been used before, also press CM

becomes the memory contents. Similarly, the "M—" key subtracts the current answer or entry from the memory contents. Example 1-10 shows how the memory works. Note that in our example, the contents of the memory is displayed only when the "memory recall" key (labeled "MR") is operated. Otherwise, the display shows the current answer or entry at all times. This type of operation is *not* universal; some memory-equipped calculators show the updated memory contents after the "M+" or "M—" key is pressed.

Because memories are not found on the majority of low-cost, four-function calculators, the procedures that follow in the text will not illustrate memory-based calculations. Before we go on, though, let's pause to illustrate the two other uses of a memory register that we mentioned a page ago:

1. Storage of a constant
2. Storage of intermediate results

In Examples 1-11 and 1-12 the "M+" key is used solely to "load" a number into memory; the number's value remains unchanged throughout the entire calculation. If your calculator has a memory, experiment to find all of its capabilities. It's a valuable computing aid!

Clearing Clearly

Most four-function calculators have two clearing keys (one labeled "C"; the other "CE"). A few machines have a single key that accomplishes both operations. Calculators with memory registers will usually also have a third "CM" key (for clearing the memory).

In general, clearing keys act as electronic erasers, that is, they "destroy" the numerical contents of the arithmetic circuitry. In particular, the "C" (or clear-all) key clears the whole calculator, and the "CE" (or clear entry) key discards only the current keyboard entry (leaving other numerical contents intact). Think of the "C" key as an eraser that wipes the whole slate clean (with the exception of the memory register, if your calculator has one) and the "CE" key as a "mistake corrector" for keyboard errors.

It is good practice to press the "C" key whenever you begin a calculation, even if your calculator automatically clears the circuitry when you turn it on (as most do). A touch on the "C" key will also "unlock" your calculator if it has "overflowed." This can happen, for example, if you multiply two six-digit numbers together on an eight-digit calculator. The product will have twelve digits, a number beyond the machine's capacity. Instantly, two things will happen: (1) The circuitry will "lock up," preventing further keyboard entry; and (2) the calculator display will indicate an overflow. To undo the log jam, simply press "C."

Example 1-11: Perform the following series of calculations sequentially:

(1) $55 \times 21 = ?$ (2) $\dfrac{100}{55} = ?$ (3) $24 + 55 = ?$

Single "=" key keyboard or dual "=" key keyboard

keyboard		display	
[C] *		0.	
[5] [5]		55.	
[M+]		55.	
[X]		55.	
[2] [1]		21.	
[=] or [+=]		1155.	*Answer 1*
[C]		0.	
[1] [0] [0]		100.	
[÷]		100.	
[MR]		55.	
[=] or [+=]		1.8181818	*Answer 2*
[C]		0.	
[2] [4]		24.	
[+] or [+=]		24.	
[MR]		55.	
[=] or [+=]		79.	*Answer 3*

*If the calculator memory has been used before, also press [CM]

The "CE" key can be used only during or immediately after the entry of a number or a mathematical command. It erases the number or command without disturbing intermediate results residing in the calculator, as shown in Example 1-13.

The second use of the "CE" key was to delete an operation command. This procedure may not work on your calculator since the "CE" key on many machines clears both the operation command

Example 1-12:   Perform the following pair of computations sequentially:

(1) $A = \dfrac{36 \times 0.3}{4}$ (2) $\dfrac{75}{A} = ?$

Single "=" key keyboard or dual "=" key keyboard

keyboard		display	
C *		0.	
3 6		36.	
X		36.	
0 . 3		0.3	
÷		10.8	
4		4.	
= or +═		2.7	*Answer*
M+		2.7	
C		0.	
7 5		75.	
÷		75.	
MR		2.7	
= or +═		27.777777	*Answer*

*If the calculator memory has been used earlier, also press [CM]

and the previously entered number, essentially bringing you back to the starting point of your calculation.

In the interest of saving cost and space, a few calculators have a single dual-function clearing key labeled "CE/C."* This can be a tricky device to master! Your first push on the key performs the "CE" function; the second touch "clears-all." You need a steady finger to correct keying errors without disturbing other numerical contents. Note that a few "price leader" calculators do not provide the "CE" function at all; with these a keying error means starting all over again.

*Occasionally, this dual-function key may just be labeled "C."

Example 1-13:   Perform the following computation:

$$\frac{24 \times 2.5 \times 15}{75} = ?$$

Single "=" key keyboard or dual "=" key keyboard

	keyboard			display
C				0.
2	6	ERROR 1		26.
CE				0.
2	4			24.
÷		ERROR 2		24.
CE				24.
X				24.
2	.	5		2.5
X				60.
1	5			15.
÷				900.
5	9	ERROR 3		59.
CE				900.
7	5			75.
=	or	+=		12.

With few exceptions, the "C" or "CE" keys *do not* affect memory-register contents on memory-equipped calculators. The memory is cleared by a separate "CM" key. This arrangement permits you to perform any desired sequence of calculations—each preceded by a "C" operation—without disturbing the number stored in memory. (Of course, the contents of the memory register will be lost if you turn the calculator off.)

Hints for More Efficient Calculating

There's more than one way to skin a cat and also to perform most complicated arithmetic computations: Some ways are more *efficient* than others. As a rule, efficient computation procedures accomplish the following:

1. Take fewer keystrokes to get the job done
2. Involve fewer "scratchpad transfers" (when you write an intermediate result down on paper, then re-enter it later during the calculation)
3. Involve simpler scratchpad transfers (that is, simpler numbers)

Efficiency is worthwhile for one fundamental reason: Eliminating unnecessary keystrokes and/or complex scratchpad transfers helps reduce the prime source of calculation errors, namely, careless mistakes while keying-in numbers.

Simply stated, the key to efficient operation is *planning.* You should think a bit about complex calculations before you pick up your machine. Obviously, there is a "break-even point." It doesn't make sense to overplan a computation to the point where you spend more time thinking efficiently than you would spend calculating inefficiently! Experience using your calculator will help you find the happy middle ground.

We'll conclude this introductory chapter with Example 1-14, a handful of "wrong way/right way" computations that illustrate the art of computation planning. Actually, all of the examples demonstrate the validity of one simple calculating rule: *Whenever possible, perform sequences of similar arithmetic operations together and avoid mixing assorted multiplications and divisions with additions and subtractions.*

Example 1-14: Perform the following series of computations:

(1) $\dfrac{1}{2} + \dfrac{3}{4} + \dfrac{5}{20} = \ ?$

(2) $\dfrac{1}{8} \times \dfrac{2}{12} \times \dfrac{3}{4} = \ ?$

(3) $36 + 15 + (9 \times 12) = \ ?$

(4) $\dfrac{4 + 8}{2 \times 36} = \ ?$

Note: The procedures that follow will work on both single "=" key calculators and dual "=" key machines. On several occasions, clearing operations (that is, pressing the "C" key) and accompanying *scratchpad transfers* (that is, jotting down, then reentering intermediate results) have been used that may not be necessary when the computations are performed on your calculator. These have been incorporated to insure that the procedures will work on calculators equipped for "automatic constant" operation. For convenience, these possibly extraneous steps have been marked with asterisks.

Computation 1—Right Way

keyboard		display
C		0.
1		1.
÷		1.
2		2.
= or +=		0.5
SCRATCHPAD TRANSFER		0.5
C *		0.
3		3.
÷		3.
4		4.
= or +=		0.75
SCRATCHPAD TRANSFER		0.75
C *		0.
5		5.
÷		5.
2 0		20.
+ or +=		0.25
SCRATCHPAD TRANSFER*		0.25
C *		0.
REENTER . 2 5		0.25

[+] or [+=]		0.25
REENTER [.] [7] [5]		0.75
[+] or [+=]		1.
REENTER [.] [5]		0.5
[=] or [+=]		1.5

Computation 1—Wrong Way

keyboard	display
[C]	0.
[1]	1.
[÷]	1.
[2]	2.
[=] or [+=]	0.5
SCRATCHPAD TRANSFER	0.5
[C] *	0.
[3]	3.
[÷]	3.
[4]	4.
[=] or [+=]	0.75
SCRATCHPAD TRANSFER	0.75
[C]	0
REENTER [0] [.] [5]	0.5
[+] or [+=]	0.5
REENTER [0] [.] [7] [5]	0.75
[=] or [+=]	1.25
SCRATCHPAD TRANSFER	1.25

keyboard	display
5	5.
÷	5.
2 0	20.
+ or +═	0.25
SCRATCHPAD TRANSFER*	0.25
C *	0.25
REENTER . 2 5	0.25
+ or +═	0.25
1 . 2 5	1.25
= or +═	1.5

Computation 2—Right Way

keyboard	display
1	1.
÷	1.
8	8.
×	0.125
2	2.
÷	0.25
1 2	12.
×	0.0208333
3	3.
÷	0.0624999
4	4.
= or +═	0.0156249

Computation 2—Wrong Way

keyboard	display
[1]	1.
[÷]	1.
[8]	8.
[=] or [+=]	0.125
SCRATCHPAD TRANSFER	0.125
[C] *	0.
[2]	2.
[÷]	2.
[1] [2]	12.
[=] or [+=]	0.1666666
SCRATCHPAD TRANSFER	0.1666666
[C] *	0.
[3]	3.
[÷]	3.
[4]	4.
[=] or [+=]	0.75
SCRATCHPAD TRANSFER*	0.75
[C] *	0.
REENTER [.] [7] [5]	0.75
[X]	0.75
REENTER [.] [1] [6] [6] [6] [6] [6] [6]	0.1666666
[X]	0.1249999
REENTER [.] [1] [2] [5]	0.125
[=] or [+=]	0.0156249

Computation 3—Right Way

	keyboard			display
	C			0.
	9			9.
	×			9.
	1	2		12.
	+	or	+≡	108.
	SCRATCHPAD TRANSFER*			108.
	C *			0.
REENTER	1	0	8	108.
	+	or	+≡	108.
	3	6		36.
	+	or	+≡	144.
	1	5		15.
	=	or	+≡	159.

Computation 3—Wrong Way

	keyboard			display
	C			0.
	3	6		36.
	+	or	+≡	36.
	1	5		15.
	=	or	+≡	51.
	SCRATCHPAD TRANSFER			51.
	9			9.
	×			9.
	1	2		12.

keyboard	display
$\boxed{+}$ or $\boxed{+=}$	108.
SCRATCHPAD TRANSFER*	108.
$\boxed{C}$ *	0.
REENTER $\boxed{1}$ $\boxed{0}$ $\boxed{8}$	108.
$\boxed{+}$ or $\boxed{+=}$	108.
REENTER $\boxed{5}$ $\boxed{1}$	51.
$\boxed{=}$ or $\boxed{+=}$	159.

Computation 4—Right Way

keyboard	display
$\boxed{C}$	0.
$\boxed{4}$	4.
$\boxed{+}$ or $\boxed{+=}$	4.
$\boxed{8}$	8.
$\boxed{=}$ or $\boxed{+=}$	12.
$\boxed{\div}$	12.
$\boxed{2}$	2.
$\boxed{\div}$	6.
$\boxed{3}$ $\boxed{6}$	36.
$\boxed{=}$ or $\boxed{+=}$	0.1666666

Computation 4—Wrong Way

keyboard	display
$\boxed{C}$	0.
$\boxed{2}$	2.
$\boxed{\times}$	2.
$\boxed{3}$ $\boxed{6}$	36.

$=$ or $+=$		72.
SCRATCHPAD TRANSFER		72.
C *		0.
4		4.
+ or $+=$		4.
8		8.
= or $+=$		12.
÷		12.
REENTER 7 2		72.
= or $+=$		0.1666666

2
Flowcharts
and Algorithms

An *algorithm* is simply a procedure for solving a specific arithmetic or mathematical problem. It is a word that is popular among computer programmers—the first step in writing a computer program is creating an algorithm—and it belongs in the vocabulary of everyone who owns an electronic calculator. The pages that follow contain a comprehensive collection of algorithms—mathematical "recipes" for scores of different familiar computations.

Is an algorithm the same thing as a formula? Not really! A formula is a statement—written in mathematical shorthand—that says *what* must be done. An algorithm explains *how* to do it.

It is usually possible to create several different algorithms for any given problem. The algorithms that follow are each *one* way of tackling a specific problem. You probably will invent other ways— and create other algorithms—as you gain experience with your calculator.

A *flow chart* is a convenient graphical method for describing an algorithm. The old saw "one picture is worth ten thousand words" is especially meaningful when we talk about algorithms. Sure, it's possible to describe an algorithm with words: "Add factor A to factor B; then subtract factor C; then multiply this answer by 4.67," for example. But a flow chart does the job better and is much easier to understand—once you get the hang of it.

You'll observe from Figure 2-1 that a flow chart is constructed out of a number of different geometric shapes that are linked together with arrows. Each shape represents a specific *kind* of calculator operation (we'll say more about this shortly). You "read"

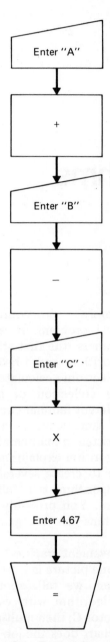

Figure 2-1 Typical flow chart

a flow chart by starting at the top, then following the arrows down to the bottom. Think of the flow chart as a "road map," with each "town" on the map a specific calculator operation.

Broadly speaking, there are four categories of different operations you perform when you solve a problem on a calculator. To make the flow charts easier to understand, each category—or kind—of operation has its own special shape. These are illustrated in Fig. 2-2: **1940672**

1. *Arithmetic operations*, that is, "+", "−", "X", and "÷", are indicated by an ordinary rectangle. Simply stated, a rectangle tells you to press one of the four function keys.

2. *Manual control operations*, that is, "Clear" and "=" (or "+=" and "−=") are shown with a keystone shape. A minor point of confusion occurs here for owners of dual-equals key calculators: Because the "+=" and "−=" keys also perform arithmetic operations (specifically, addition and subtraction) as well as serve as "=" keys, they may also be shown in ordinary rectangles in those procedure examples specifically designed for dual-equals key machines.

3. *Data input*, that is, the entering of problem numbers and constants, is indicated by a ramp-shaped block.

4. *Scratchpad transfer*, that is, jotting down an "intermediate result" on a piece of paper, is denoted by a "tilted" rectangle.

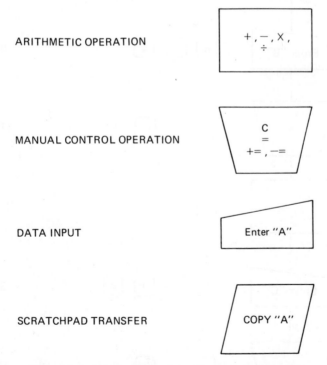

ARITHMETIC OPERATION $+, -, X, \div$

MANUAL CONTROL OPERATION   C = += , −=

DATA INPUT   Enter "A"

SCRATCHPAD TRANSFER   COPY "A"

Figure 2-2 Shapes categorizing flow chart operations

All of the algorithms in this volume will be constructed of these four "building block" shapes, or, more accurately, the flow charts that map the algorithms will be made of these shapes.

The numerical example that illustrates each procedure is presented to the right of each flow chart. The example consists of two columns: the first column represents the keys to be pressed; the second column shows the calculator display that results from pressing the keys.

Here, for example, is the algorithm and numerical example for solving Z = (A + B) / C when A = 25, B = 6.4, and C = 3.14.

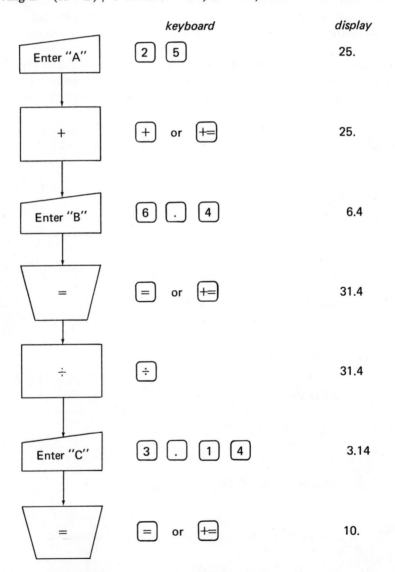

	keyboard	*display*
Enter "A"	2 5	25.
+	+ or +=	25.
Enter "B"	6 . 4	6.4
=	= or +=	31.4
÷	÷	31.4
Enter "C"	3 . 1 4	3.14
=	= or +=	10.

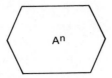

NUMBER "A" RAISED TO POWER "n"

Figure 2-3 Shape for raising a number to a power

Several of the financial algorithm flow charts include a fifth shape—a six-sided block—that represents the arithmetic operation of raising a number to a power. As described on page 94, this operation involves a series of repetitive multiplications using the calculator's "constant multiplication" feature. Broadly speaking, this block (see Fig. 2-3) is only used when the power is a large number; calculations involving squared or cubed factors are diagrammed in their entirety.

3
To Round
or Not to Round?

A long string of digits lighting up your calculator's display doesn't necessarily mean an "accurate" answer. Often, many of the digits you see are meaningless and should be discarded by rounding off the answer.

If a financial calculation yields an answer of $175.94321, it's fairly obvious that the answer must be rounded to $175.94. But, what do you do if an estimate of the volume of concrete in a patio turns out to be 2.015625 cubic yards? Or if the estimate of the travel time of a bullet from gun to target is 0.114321 seconds? Or if your calculation "proves" that an electrical appliance draws 3.52179 amperes of current? Do the numbers mean anything?

Simply stated, you can't get anything more out of a calculation than you put into it. Thus, the first step in deciding how many answer digits to keep is to look carefully at the *precision* of the numbers and constants you've used to perform the arithmetic. The precision of your final answer should reflect the precision of the input numbers.

Consider the electrical appliance example as an illustration. The algorithm for calculating current draw (on page 81) uses the power line voltage as one of the input variables. But, the actual power line voltage may vary *a few percent* from the "nominal" 120 volts ac. The "answer" mentioned above has five decimal places, which assumes an accuracy far beyond a few percent. By rounding the display answer off to 3.5 amperes, we can bring it into line with the facts of electrical life.

Unfortunately, there are no magic rules to follow. You must learn to examine each set of input numbers and then decide how precise an answer they can sustain. We've done just that in the numerical examples in this book.

There is another factor to consider. Even if the answer is potentially accurate, does it have any meaning? For example, if you used a very precise ruler—say one with gradations down to 1/64 inch—to measure your new patio area, you might plausibly decide that you needed 2.015625 cubic yards of concrete to complete the job. But, where on earth would you buy *exactly* 2.015625 yards of concrete. Your answer is precise to within individual *drops* of wet concrete. Obviously, it would make more sense to ask the concrete supplier to deliver 2 cubic yards. Here again, whenever appropriate, we have rounded off silly answers to make them sensible answers. You should always do the same!

The algorithms that follow in the next five sections will not necessarily be the most efficient computing procedures for your particular model calculator. There are two reasons for this:

1. Each algorithm has been designed to be a *universal* procedure, a sequence of operations that will work on all popular four-function machines, including those models equipped with an "automatic constant" feature.

2. Each algorithm has been designed to be as understandable as possible. Often the most efficient procedure is difficult to grasp because its "dovetailed" operations may seem illogical.

The point is this: Use the presented algorithm the first time you tackle a new problem, but be sure to experiment to find a more efficient procedure if you will be performing the computation again and again.

4

Money and Finance

Mortgage Payment Calculation

This simple procedure—and the accompanying table—will enable you to compute the monthly payment for any 20, 25, or 30-year mortgage whose interest rate ranges between 5 and 12 percent. The computed payment represents the monthly interest and principal; it does not include taxes, insurance, sewer fees, etc., that may also be paid to the bank on a monthly basis.

$$\text{Monthly payment} = M/A$$

where M = total value of mortgage (in dollars) and A = conversion factor (from Table 4-1). *Note:* The interest rates shown in the table are expressed in decimal fractions. Use the procedure on page 93 to convert percentage rates to decimal fractions.)

EXAMPLE 4-1: What is the monthly payment on a 25-year mortgage for $36,750 at an interest rate of 9.75 percent? *Answer:* $327.49.

keyboard	display
Enter "M" 3 6 7 5 0	36750.
÷	
÷	36750.

No. of years	Interest rate	Conversion factor	No. of years	Interest rate	Conversion factor
20	.07	128.983	25	.0975	112.216
20	.0725	126.522	25	.1	110.047
20	.075	124.132	25	.1025	107.947
20	.0775	121.81	25	.105	105.912
20	.08	119.554	25	.1075	103.94
20	.0825	117.362	25	.11	102.029
20	.085	115.231	25	.1125	100.176
20	.0875	113.159	25	.115	98.3798
20	.09	111.145	25	.1175	96.6372
20	.0925	109.186	25	.12	94.9466
20	.095	107.281	30	.05	186.282
20	.0975	105.428	30	.0525	181.093
20	.1	103.625	30	.055	176.122
20	.1025	101.87	30	.0575	171.358
20	.105	100.162	30	.06	166.792
20	.1075	98.4999	30	.0625	162.412
20	.11	96.8815	30	.065	158.211
20	.1125	95.3056	30	.0675	154.179
20	.115	93.7708	30	.07	150.308
20	.1175	92.2759	30	.0725	146.59
20	.12	90.8194	30	.075	143.018
25	.05	171.06	30	.0775	139.584
25	.0525	166.876	30	.08	136.283

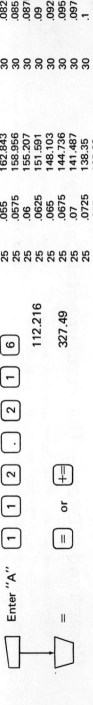

Enter "A" [1] [1] [2] [.] [2] [1] [6]

112.216

[=] or [+=]   327.49

Table 4-1 Conversion Table

No. of years	Interest rate	Conversion factor	No. of years	Interest rate	Conversion factor
20	.05	151.525	20	.06	139.581
20	.0525	148.402	20	.0625	136.812
20	.055	145.373	20	.065	134.125
20	.0575	142.433	20	.0675	131.516

No. of years	Interest rate	Conversion factor	No. of years	Interest rate	Conversion factor
25	.055	162.843	30	.0825	133.109
25	.0575	158.956	30	.085	130.054
25	.06	155.207	30	.0875	127.113
25	.0625	151.591	30	.09	124.282
25	.065	148.103	30	.0925	121.555
25	.0675	144.736	30	.095	118.927
25	.07	141.487	30	.0975	116.394
25	.0725	138.35	30	.1	113.951
25	.075	135.32	30	.1025	111.595
25	.0775	132.393	30	.105	109.321
25	.08	129.565	30	.1075	107.126
25	.0825	126.831	30	.11	105.006
25	.085	124.289	30	.1125	102.959
25	.0875	121.633	30	.115	100.98
25	.09	119.162	30	.1175	99.0678
25	.0925	116.77	30	.12	97.2183
25	.095	114.456			

The Consumer Price Index

The *consumer price index* (or CPI) is a convenient arithmetic device to demonstrate the effects of inflation. It is a carefully contrived average that can be used to compare the buying power of today's money with the buying power of money during a "base year" in the past. For example, suppose the current CPI is quoted as 163.2 (1967 base). This means that 163.2 of today's cents will buy about as much as 100 cents back in 1967.

You can use the CPI to gauge the worth of today's money in terms of the base year's dollars and cents. The following formula yields the number of base-year dollars that is equivalent—in buying power—to a specified number of today's dollars:

$$\$B = (\$T \times 100) / CPI$$

where $\$B$ = base-year dollars, $\$T$ = today's dollars, and CPI = consumer price index.

EXAMPLE 4-2: What is the buying power of $10,000 today, compared to 1967 dollars, assuming that today's CPI equals 154.5 (1967 base). *Answer:* $6472.49 worth of 1967 dollars.

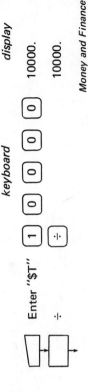

	keyboard	display
Enter "$T"	[1] [0] [0] [0] [0]	10000.
[÷]	[1] [÷]	10000.

100.

6472.4919

Enter "CPI" [1] [5] [4] [.] [5]   154.5

× [5]   64.724919

Enter 100 [1] [0] [0]   =   or   [+=]   6472.4919

100.

Simple Interest

Simple interest is a straight "rental fee" for money paid to a lender (by a borrower) or to a saver (by a bank). Usually, simple interest is paid only on short-term financial transactions—most often less than one year long. The following formula yields the simple interest payment for a given principal that is lent (borrowed) for a specific period of time.

$$I = \frac{P \times N \times R}{100}$$

where P = principal (in dollars), N = time period (in years; N = 0.5 for 6 months, etc.), and R = interest rate per year (in percent).

EXAMPLE 4-3: Compute the simple interest payment on a loan of $4500, lent for a period of nine months at an annual interest rate of 7 percent per year. *Answer:* $236.25.

keyboard	display
Enter "P" [4] [5] [0] [0]	4500.
÷	4500.
Enter 100 [1] [0] [0]	100.
×	100.
Enter "N" [.] [7] [5]	0.75
×	33.75
Enter "R" [7]	7.
= or [+=]	236.25

Compound Interest—The Fundamental Calculation

This procedure is one of the most important financial computations, both in its own right and as the basis of the more complex calculations that follow. The formula presented below computes the growth of a lump sum of money deposited in a

percent. You can usually do this "by eye"—for example, 7 percent is equivalent to 0.07, and 1.2 percent is equivalent to 0.012. However, for convenience, we have presented a simple algorithm that let's your calculator do the work, on page 93.

savings account, or the total to be repaid on a single-payment loan.

Compound interest differs from simple interest in that the accrued interest is added to the principal at the end of each *compounding period*. Thus, the principal grows at a much faster pace than in a simple-interest transaction. The calculation yields the *compound amount*, "A," (the total sum of principal and interest) rather than just the dollar amount of the interest:

$$A = P \times (1 + R)N$$

where A = compound amount (in dollars), P = principal (in dollars), R = interest rate *per compounding period* (expressed as a decimal fraction), and N = number of compounding periods.

It is vital that you understand the meanings of "interest rate per compounding period," and "number of compounding periods" before you begin an actual calculation. This is because compounding and interest accruing often take place *more* than once a year although interest rate is usually quoted on a yearly basis (e.g., 6-percent, or 0.06, per year). Hence the interest per compounding period is lower than the yearly interest, whereas the number of compounding periods is greater than the number of years.

For example, if a savings bank pays 6 percent a year interest compounded quarterly (every three months), the interest per compounding period is 1.5 percent, or 0.015 (6 ÷ 4 = 1.5), and there are four compounding periods per year. We've presented two complete examples (Examples 4-4 and 4-5), both using identical algorithms, to illustrate yearly and oftener-than-yearly compounding.

One final point: The interest rate per compounding period, "R", must be expressed as a decimal fraction rather than as a

EXAMPLE 4-4: $7000 is deposited in a savings account that pays interest at the rate of 6 percent (0.06) compounded *yearly* (one compounding period per year). What is the compound amount—principal plus interest—after five years? *Answer:* $9367.58. *Note:* See page 94 for the algorithm for raising a number to a power (indicated on the flow chart by a six-sided block).

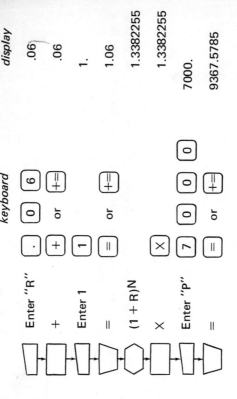

	keyboard	display
Enter "R"	. 0 6 or +=	.06 / .06
+	+ or =	
Enter 1	1	
=	=	1.
(1 + R)N		1.06
×	×	1.3382255
Enter "p"	7 0 0 0	1.3382255
=	= or +=	7000.
		9367.5785

EXAMPLE 4-5: $4600 is deposited in a savings account that pays interest at the rate of 8 percent (0.08) compounded *quarterly* (four compounding periods per year). What is the compound amount after 10 years? Here, there are a total of 40 compounding periods, and the interest rate per compound period is 2 percent (0.02). *Answer:* $10,156.97.

Money and Finance

The algorithm is identical to the one presented above:

keyboard	display
1	1.
+ or +≡	1.
.02	.02
= or +≡	1.02

keyboard	display
X	Compute $(1.02)^{40}$ — 2.2080373
	2.2080373
4 6 0 0 or +≡	4600.
= or +≡	10156.971

44

Effective Interest Rate

When interest is compounded more than once a year (when there are two or more compound periods per year), the effective—or actual—annual interest rate is slightly higher than the quoted annual rate. Simply stated, this means that the *compound amount* (or principal plus interest) at the end of one year is a bit greater than the compound amount that would be produced by once-per-year compounding. The formula for the effective rate—expressed as a decimal fraction—is:

$$R_e = (1 + R)^N - 1$$

where R_e = effective interest rate per compounding period, R = interest rate per compounding period (expressed as a decimal fraction), and N = number of compounding periods per year. *Note:* Please read the previous section for exact definitions of R and N. To convert R_e into a percentage value, multiply by 100.

EXAMPLE 4-6: The quoted interest on a savings account is 6 percent a year (0.06) compounded quarterly, so that N = 4 and R = 0.015 (0.06 ÷ 4). What is the effective annual interest? *Answer:*

R_e = 0.0614 (or 6.14 percent). *Note:* See page 94 for the algorithm for raising a number to a power (indicated on the flow chart by a six-sided block).

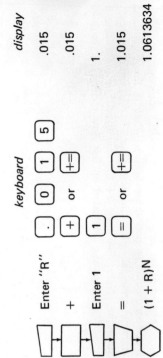

	keyboard	display
Enter "R"	. 0 1 5	.015
+	+ or +≡	.015
Enter 1	1	1.
=	= or +≡	1.015
$(1 + R)^N$		1.0613634
Subtract 1 to yield answer		0.0613634

Savings Account Calculation—Periodic Deposit

This procedure estimates the total amount of money (principal plus interest) you will accumulate in a savings account over a number of years as you make periodic deposits into the account. The estimate will be exact if you deposit money once each year; it will be slightly high if you make weekly or monthly deposits into the account. For maximum accuracy, use the *effective interest rate* (see the previous section) in the calculation rather than the quoted interest rate. Here is the formula:

$$C = \frac{D \times [(1+R)^Y - 1]}{R}$$

where D = total yearly deposit (in dollars), Y = number of years, R = yearly interest rate (expressed as a decimal fraction), and C = compound amount (principal plus interest, in dollars). If you plan to make weekly or monthly deposits, calculate the total amount that will be deposited per year. Use this figure for "D".

EXAMPLE 4-7: How much money will accumulate in a savings account that pays 6 percent per year interest, compounded quarterly (effective interest = 0.0614), when $100 a month is deposited regularly for ten years? Here, D = $1200 per year. *Answer:* $15921.32. *Note:* See page 94 for the algorithm for raising a number to a power (indicated on the flow chart by a six-sided block).

PART 1

Enter "R"	keyboard	display
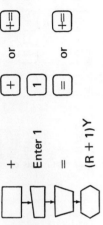	. 0 6 1 4	.0614

(R + 1)Y   +   or   +=
   Enter 1   1
   =   or   +=

| .0614 |
| 1. |
| 1.0614 |
| 1.8146409 |

Subtract 1 from answer and enter below

PART 2

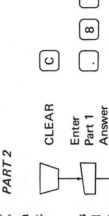

CLEAR   C   0.

Enter Part 1 Answer   . 8 1 4 6 4 0 9   0.8146409

×   ×   0.8146409

Enter "D"   1 2 0 0   1200.

÷   ÷   977.56908

Enter "R"   . 0 6 1 4   .0614

=   or   +=   15921.32

Savings Account Calculation—Desired Accumulation

This procedure estimates the amount of money you must deposit yearly into a savings account in order to accumulate a given *compound amount* (principal plus interest) over a specific number of years. The answer will be slightly low if you deposit the yearly total in a series of weekly or monthly deposits into the account. For maximum accuracy, use the *effective interest rate* (see page 44) in the calculation rather than the quoted interest rate. Here is the formula:

$$D = \frac{R \times C}{(1+R)^Y - 1}$$

where D = total yearly deposit (in dollars), Y = number of years, C = compound amount (in dollars), R = yearly interest rate (expressed as a decimal fraction). Since the answer "D" is the total yearly deposit, you can calculate the equivalent monthly or weekly deposit by dividing the answer by 12 or 52, respectively.

EXAMPLE 4-8: How much money must be deposited into a savings account each year for ten years to accumulate a total of $18,000 if the account pays 6 percent interest per year (effective interest 0.0614)? *Answer:* $1356.67. *Note:* See page 94 for the algorithm for raising a number to a power (indicated on the flow chart by a six-sided block).

PART 1

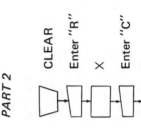

	keyboard				display
Enter "R"	.	0	6	1	4	.0614

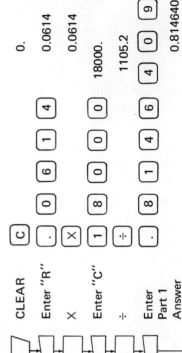

+	or	+
Enter 1		1
=	or	=
$(R+1)^Y$		

.0614

1.

1.0614

1.8146409

Subtract 1 from answer and enter below

PART 2

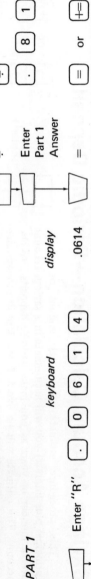

				display
CLEAR	C			0.
Enter "R"	.	0	6	1	4	0.0614
×	×			0.0614
Enter "C"	1	8	0	0	0	18000.
÷	÷			1105.2
Enter Part 1 Answer	.	8	1	4	6	4	0	9	0.8146409
=	or	=		1356.6713

46

"Perpetual Annuity"

You can establish a "perpetual annuity" by depositing a sum of money in a savings account and then withdrawing only the interest payments each year. The bank balance remains constant because the interest doesn't have a chance to increase the principal into a *compound amount* (principal plus interest). This procedure yields the amount of money that must be deposited to produce a specific yearly interest payment. For accuracy, use the *effective interest rate* (see page 44) rather than the quoted interest rate. Here is the formula:

$$P = \frac{I}{R}$$

where P = required principal deposit (in dollars), I = desired yearly interest payment (in dollars), and R = yearly interest rate (expressed as a decimal fraction).

EXAMPLE 4-9: How much money must be deposited in a savings account that pays 6 percent a year, compounded quarterly (effective interest = 0.0614) to yield a "perpetual annuity" of $1500 per year? *Answer:* $24,429.97.

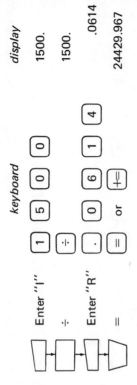

keyboard	display
Enter "I" 1 5 0 0	1500.
÷	1500.
Enter "R" . 0 6 1 4	.0614
= or +≡	24429.967

Estimating the True Interest of a Loan

The Federal "Truth-in-Lending" Act requires that a borrower be told the true annual interest of an installment loan or time-payment plan. This formula will let you do your own estimating even before you start signing papers. Keep in mind that the result of this procedure is only an *estimate*. The answer, a percentage expressed as a decimal fraction, represents the percentage of the *total cost of the loan* that you need not pay. Here is the formula:

$$R_t = \frac{2 \times \text{Cost}}{N \times (\text{Proceeds} + \text{Payment})}$$

where R_t = true interest rate; Proceeds = total amount of money you receive, or the value of the purchased goods (in dollars); N = number of monthly payments; Payment = monthly payment (in dollars); Cost = the total cost to you of the loan (in dollars).

You can compute the total "Cost" by adding up the total number of "Payment" dollars you will pay to the lending institution and then subtracting the "Proceeds." For example, a car loan for $3000 might be repaid in 36 installments of $100. The total amount paid to the bank is $3600 (36 × $100), and the Proceeds is $3000. Thus, the Cost of the loan is $600.

EXAMPLE 4-10: An installment loan for $4000 will be paid back in 36 installments of $135. Estimate the true interest. Here, the Cost of the loan is $860 ($4860 − $4000). *Answer:* 0.116. *Note:* To convert the answer to a percentage, multiply by 100. For this example, the result is 11.6 percent.

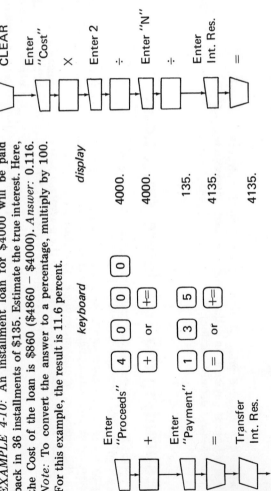

	keyboard	display
Enter "Proceeds"	4 0 0 0	4000.
+	+ or +=	4000.
Enter "Payment"	1 3 5	135.
=	= or +=	4135.
Transfer Int. Res.		4135.

	keyboard	display
CLEAR	C	0.
Enter "Cost"	8 6 0	860.
×	×	860.
Enter 2	2	2.
÷	÷	1720.
Enter "N"	3 6	36.
÷	÷	47.777777
Enter Int. Res.	4 1 3 5	4135.
=	= or +=	0.0115544

Estimating Early-Payment Rebate on an Installment Loan

Let's say that you have made 30 out of 36 payments on an installment loan, and now you would like to pay off the outstanding balance in one lump sum. How much should you pay the lending institution? Because you are paying off the loan early, the remaining balance will be less than the sum of the six remaining payments. This procedure let's you estimate how much less. It is called the "rule of 78," and it is used by many banks to compute the "rebate" due back to you for early payment. The answer is a percentage expressed as a decimal fraction; it

EXAMPLE 4-11: What is the rebate on an installment loan that calls for 36 equal payments of $75 when nine payments remain to be made and where the cost is $300? *Answer:* $R = 0.0676$. Thus, the payoff $= (9 \times \$75) - (0.0675 \times \$300) = \$675 - \$20.28 = \$654.72$.

	keyboard	display
Enter "U"	9	9.

represents the percentage of *the sum of the remaining payments* that you need not pay. Here is the formula:

$$R = \frac{U \times (U + 1)}{N \times (N + 1)}$$

where R = percentage rebate of remaining payment total, U = number of payments remaining to be paid, and N = total number of payments.

To estimate the rebate in dollars, simply multiply the total cost of the loan by R. The total sum you still owe the bank (the "payoff" figure) is:

$$\text{Payoff} = (U \times P) - (R \times \text{Cost})$$

where U and R are the quantities previously defined and P = monthly payment (in dollars).

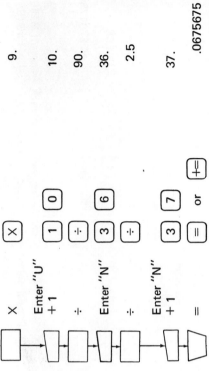

×	9.
Enter "U" +1	10.
÷	90.
3 6	36.
÷	2.5
Enter "N" +1	37.
= or ÷+	.0675675
	THIS IS "R"

Foreign Exchange Conversions

It's easy to determine the value—in U.S. dollars—of a specific quantity of foreign currency, or vice versa. All you need (besides your calculator) is one of the simple algorithms presented below, and the latest *foreign exchange rate*. Exchange rates vary from day to day; you can find them listed in the *Wall Street Journal* (available at most libraries) and in many big-city newspapers.

Two pairs of conversion formulas are presented on the next page because the exchange rate for a foreign currency may be given in one of two ways:

1. The cost in U.S. cents of a single unit of foreign currency (for example, 22 cents for one French franc)
2. The number of units of foreign currency that can be purchased for one U.S. dollar (for example, 4.56 French francs per U.S. dollar).

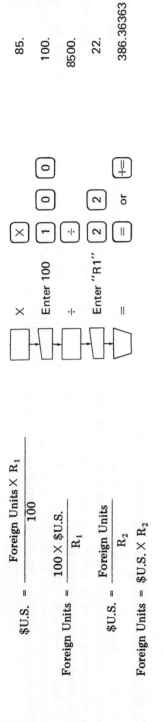

$$\$U.S. = \frac{\text{Foreign Units} \times R_1}{100}$$

$$\text{Foreign Units} = \frac{100 \times \$U.S.}{R_1}$$

$$\$U.S. = \frac{\text{Foreign Units}}{R_2}$$

$$\text{Foreign Units} = \$U.S. \times R_2$$

where R_1 = the cost in U.S. cents of a unit of foreign currency, and R_2 = the number of foreign units of currency that can be purchased for a single U.S. dollar.

EXAMPLE 4-12: What is the value in \$U.S. of 40 French francs when the cost of a single franc is \$0.22 ($R_1 = 22$)? *Answer:* \$8.80.

keyboard		display
Enter "Foreign Units"	[4] [0]	40.
[×]		40.
Enter "R1"	[2] [2]	22.
[÷]		880.
Enter 100	[1] [0] [0]	100.
[=] or [÷=]		8.8

---

	display
[×]	85.
Enter 100 [1] [0] [0]	100.
	8500.
[÷] Enter "R1" [2] [2]	22.
[=] or [÷=]	386.36363

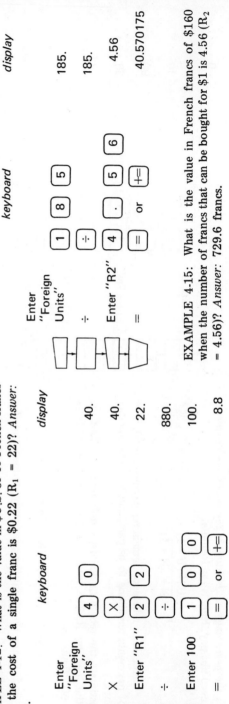

EXAMPLE 4-14: What is the value in \$U.S. of 185 French francs when the number of francs that can be bought for \$1 is 4.56 ($R_2 = 4.56$)? *Answer:* \$40.57.

keyboard		display
Enter "Foreign Units"	[1] [8] [5]	185.
[÷]		185.
Enter "R2"	[4] [.] [5] [6]	4.56
[=] or [÷=]		40.570175

EXAMPLE 4-15: What is the value in French francs of \$160 when the number of francs that can be bought for \$1 is 4.56 ($R_2 = 4.56$)? *Answer:* 729.6 francs.

keyboard		display
Enter "$US" 1 6 0		160.
×		160.
Enter "R2" 4 . 5 6		4.56
= or +=		729.6

EXAMPLE 4-13: What is the value in French francs of $85 when the cost of a single franc is $0.22 ($R_1 = 22$)? *Answer*: 386.36 francs.

keyboard	display
Enter "$US" 8 5	85.

5
Household and Workshop

Fahrenheit/Celsius Temperature Conversion

Until quite recently, the *Celsius* temperature scale was known as the *centigrade* scale. Its new name honors the Swedish astronomer who first conceived it. But labels aside, the Celsius scale is by far and away the most widely used temperature scale—at least, throughout the rest of the civilized world. In the not too distant future, the U.S., too, will adopt SI, or International System, units (the "metric system"), and the Celsius scale will become our official temperature scale.

Zero degrees Celsius (0° C) is the freezing point of water—equivalent to 32° F; 100° C is the boiling point of water (equal to 212° F). The first formula below converts degrees-F to degrees-C; the second formula reverses the process:

$$C = \frac{(F - 32) \times 5}{9}$$

$$F = \frac{9 \times C}{5} + 32$$

where C = degrees Celsius, and F = degrees Fahrenheit.

EXAMPLE 5-1: Convert 86° F to its equivalent Celsius temperature. *Answer*: 30° C.

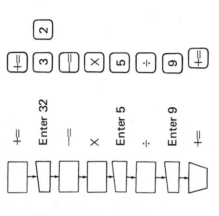

⊦≣		86.
Enter 32	3 2	32.
−≣		54.
×		54.
Enter 5	5	5.
÷		270.
Enter 9	9	9.
⊦≣		30.

EXAMPLE 5-2: Convert 20° C to its equivalent Fahrenheit temperature. *Answer*: 68° F.

keyboard	display
Enter "C" →	2 0	20.

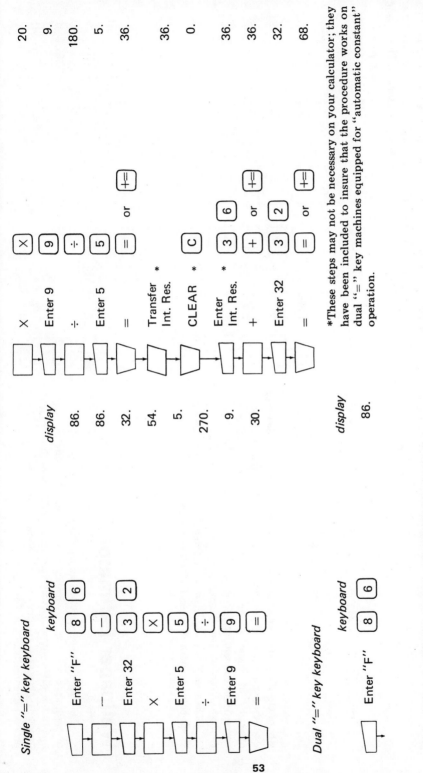

Single "=" key keyboard

keyboard

Enter "F"	8 6
-	
Enter 32	3 2
×	×
Enter 5	5
÷	÷
Enter 9	9
=	=

display
86.
86.
32.
54.
5.
270.
9.
30.

×   × 9
Enter 9
÷   ÷ 5
Enter 5
=   = or +=
Transfer Int. Res. *
CLEAR * C
Enter Int. Res. * 3 6 or +=
+ 3
Enter 32 2
= = or +=

20.
9.
180.
5.
36.
36.
0.
36.
36.
32.
68.

*These steps may not be necessary on your calculator; they have been included to insure that the procedure works on dual "=" key machines equipped for "automatic constant" operation.

Dual "=" key keyboard

keyboard

Enter "F" 8 6

display
86.

Solution Dilution Calculations

This procedure is worth its weight in saved time if you work with chemicals in liquid form—in photography, chemistry, and cooking, for example. It yields the number of *fluid ounces* of "stock solution" (of known concentration) that must be diluted

53

with water to produce a "working solution" (of desired concentration). Obviously, the stock solution must have a higher concentration than the desired working solution concentration. There are two formulas:

$$O_S = \frac{P_W \times Q}{P_S}$$

$$W = Q - O_S$$

where O_S = quantity of stock solution needed (in fluid ounces), Q = desired quantity of working solution (in fluid ounces), W = quantity of water needed (in fluid ounces), P_W = desired percentage concentration of working solution, and P_S = percentage concentration of stock solution.

When you've completed the calculations, mix O_S ounces of stock solution with W ounces of water to create the working solution.

Wallpaper Estimator

This handy procedure estimates the number of double rolls of wallpaper necessary to paper a single wall. Add the requirements for different walls together, and you'll know how much paper is necessary to decorate a room, or even a house. The procedure consists of two formulas:

EXAMPLE 5-3: How many ounces of 50-percent stock solution and how many ounces of water must be mixed together to produce 32 ounces of 18-percent working solution: *Answer:* 11.5 fluid ounces of stock solution; 20.5 fluid ounces of water. *Note:* Only the algorithm for the first formula is presented. The second formula is a simple subtraction operation.

keyboard	display
Enter "P_W" ⬚1⬚ ⬚8⬚	18.
⬚×⬚	18.
Enter "Q" ⬚3⬚ ⬚2⬚	32.
⬚÷⬚	576.
Enter "P_S" ⬚5⬚ ⬚0⬚	50.
⬚=⬚ or ⬚+=⬚	11.52
Enter "R" ⬚1⬚ ⬚0⬚	10.
⬚=⬚ or ⬚+=⬚	106.
Transfer Int. Res.	106.

$$N = \frac{8640}{W \times (H + R)}$$

$$P = \frac{S}{W \times N}$$

where N = number of "strips" of paper that will be yielded by one double roll of paper, W = width of wallpaper (in inches), H = height of wall (in inches), R = repeat length of wallpaper pattern (in inches), S = total width of wall to be papered (in inches), and P = number of double rolls needed.

This procedure takes into account the differing widths and "pattern repeat lengths" of various wallpapers. The first formula yields the number of strips of a specific paper (specific pattern and width) that can be cut from a double roll. The answer must be truncated (the fractional part ignored) before it is used in the second formula, which estimates the total number of double rolls needed to do the job.

EXAMPLE 5-4: A wall measuring 96 inches high by 240 inches wide will be covered with wallpaper. The selected paper is 20 inches wide and has a pattern repeat length of 10 inches. How many strips can be cut from each double roll and how many double rolls are required? *Answer:* Four strips per double roll; three double rolls will do the job.

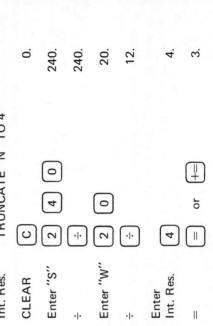

Step	Keys	display
CLEAR	C	0.
Enter 8640	8 6 4 0	8640.
÷	÷	8640.
Enter "W"	2 0	20.
÷	÷	432.
Enter Int. Res.	1 0 6	106.
=	= or +=	4.0754716

THIS IS "N"

TRUNCATE "N" TO 4

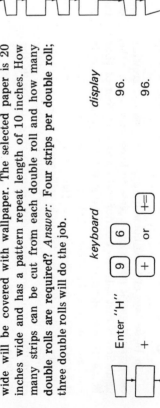

Step	Keys	display
Transfer Int. Res. CLEAR	C	0.
Enter "S"	2 4 0	240.
÷	÷	240.
Enter "W"	2 0	20.
÷	÷	20.
Enter Int. Res.	4	12.
=	= or +=	4.
		3.

keyboard	display
Enter "H" 9 6	96.
+	96.
or +=	

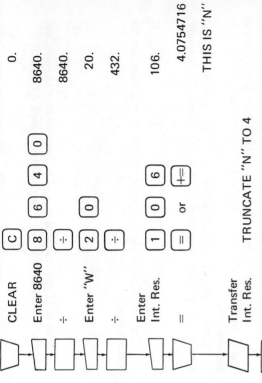

Gauging the Effectiveness of Your Home's Insulation

In these days of rising home heating fuel costs and growing energy shortages, it makes good sense to know how effective the insulation is that fills the exterior walls and attic floor of your house. Here's a detailed algorithm that will help you find out. It estimates the cost of heating your house if it had "full" insulation (typically, this means 3½ inches of glass fiber insulation in walls; 6 inches of glass fiber insulation in ceilings and floors; and storm windows or double-pane "thermal windows"). At the end of the calculations, you compare your actual yearly tab with the estimate.

Before you can begin, you will need to know several numbers that can be provided by your local heating contractor, oil company, gas company, or electric company. These are:

D = the number of *degree days* for the heating season in your area.

T_d = the *winter design temperature* in your area (in degrees F).

C_c = the total cost during heating season of cooking fuel for a family of your size (this is necessary only if you cook with the same fuel consumed by your heating system).

C_w = the total cost during heating season of heating hot water for a family of your size (this is necessary only if water is heated by the same fuel consumed by the heating system).

Step 1. Measure the following areas:

W = total area, in square feet, of walls that separate heated spaces from unheated spaces (include walls facing garages and unheated rooms). In

and L_g are computed in BTU-per-hour heat flow. To perform the calculations, you must know T, the inside/outside temperature differential. You find T by subtracting T_d (the outdoor winter design temperature) from T_t (the normal temperature or thermostat setting inside your home). Here are the four heat loss formulas:

$$L_w = W \times T \times 0.07$$
$$L_f = F \times T \times 0.05$$
$$L_c = R \times T \times 0.05$$
$$L_g = G \times T \times 1.10$$

Note: If the house is built over a heated basement, set L_f equal to 0; if the house is built over an unheated basement or crawl space, divide the above answer for L_f by 2 before you use it in the next step.

Step 4. Add the individual heat loss figures together to yield a total BTU-per-hour heat loss, L, from the house. The formula:

$$L = L_w + L_f + L_c + L_g$$

Step 5. Calculate the estimated fuel bill, E, in dollars, for the heating season:

$$E = \frac{L \times 24 \times H}{100,000 \times T}$$

Step 6. If you use heating fuel to heat water or to cook, add "typical" costs C_c and C_w to yield a total estimated fuel bill:

$$E_t = E + C_w + C_c$$

most cases, W will be the total exterior wall area of the house.

G = total area, in square feet, of outside windows and doors.

R = total area, in square feet, of top-floor ceiling.

F = total area, in square feet, of ground-floor floor.

Step 2. Calculate the "heating index," H, for your locale. To do this, you must know F, the cost of a single unit of fuel or energy in your area. If you heat with oil, F should be the cost (in *dollars*) of one gallon of oil; if you heat with gas, F should be the cost (in *dollars*) of 1000-cubic feet of gas; if you heat with electricity, F should be the cost (in *dollars*) of one kilowatt-hour of electricity. For example, F might be $0.35 a gallon for oil, $0.32 per 1000-cubic feet for gas, and $0.03 per kilowatt-hour for electricity. Use one of the following formulas to calculate H:

For oil heat:

$$H = \frac{D \times F}{0.99}$$

For gas heat:

$$H = \frac{D \times F}{0.8}$$

For electric heat:

$$H = D \times F \times 20.75$$

Step 3. Calculate the heat loss per hour through the walls, floor, ceiling, and windows. Each of the four losses—L_W, L_f, L_c,

EXAMPLE 5-5: Estimate the cost of heating a fully insulated house that has a 1,500-sq ft external wall area, 1,400-sq ft ceiling and floor areas, and a 200-sq ft exterior glass and door area. The house is built on a slab and has a gas-fired furnace that provides heat only (C_W and C_C both equal 0). The local heating season has an average of 5500 degree days, and the outside winter design temperature is 10°F. The cost of gas is $0.30 per 1000 cu ft. The thermostat is set at 70°F. *Answer:* $230.18.

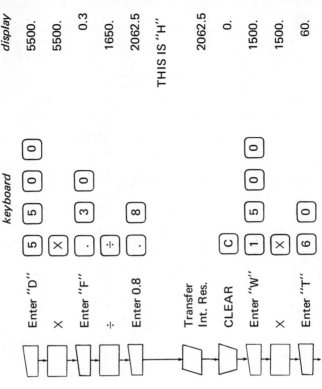

	keyboard	display
Enter "D"	5 5 0 0	5500.
×	×	5500.
Enter "F"	. 3 0	0.3
÷	÷	1650.
Enter 0.8	. 8	2062.5
Transfer Int. Res.		THIS IS "H"
		2062.5
CLEAR	C	0.
Enter "W"	1 5 0 0	1500.
×	×	1500.
Enter "T"	6 0	60.

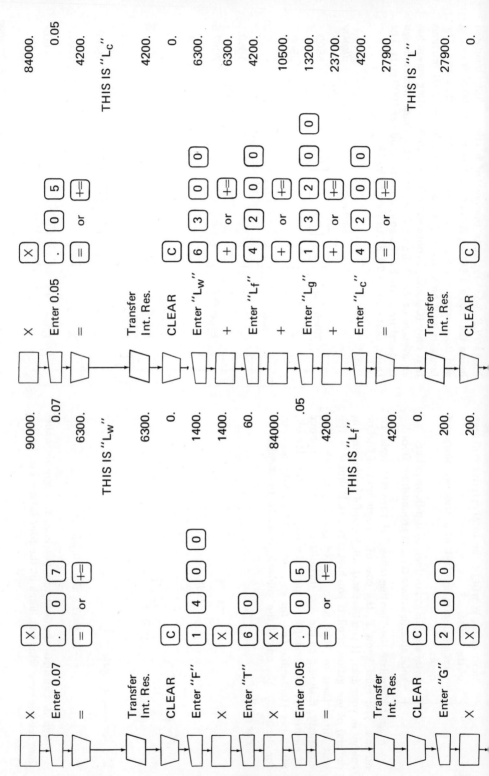

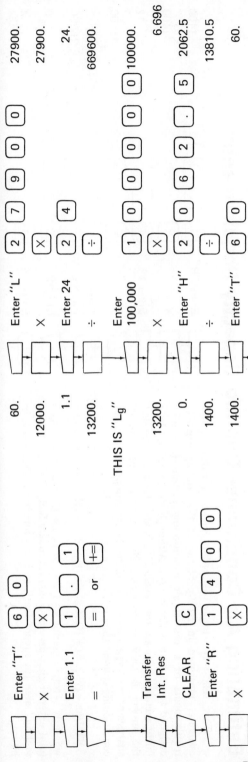

Air Conditioner Rating Conversion

The cooling capacity of an air conditioner may be specified either in terms of a BTU-per hour rating or a tonnage rating. The BTU (British Thermal Unit) is a measure of heat. Thus, a BTU-per-hour rating specifies the amount of heat that an air conditioner can remove from a house (or room) during one hour or operation. Most new machines will carry such a rating.

In years past, it was common to specify air conditioner cooling capacity in terms of a tonnage rating ("tons"). A so-called "1-ton" air conditioner will remove as much heat in 24 hours as will be absorbed by one ton of ice melting in 24 hours. The BTU-per-hour rating, B, and tonnage rating, T, can be interconverted with the use of the following formulas:

$$B = T \times 11967$$

$$T = B / 11967$$

EXAMPLE 5-6: What is the BTU-per-hour rating of a "3-ton" central air conditioning system? *Answer:* 35,901 BTU-per-hour.

keyboard	display
Enter "T" [3] [×]	3.
Enter 11967 [1] [9] [6] [7]	11967.
[=] or [+=]	35901.

EXAMPLE 5-7: What is the tonnage rating of a room air conditioner rated to remove 7,500 BTU-per-hour? *Answer:* 0.63 tons.

keyboard	display
Enter "B" [7] [5] [0] [0] [÷]	7500.
	7500.
Enter 11967 [1] [9] [6] [7]	11967.
[=] or [+=]	0.6267234

Estimating Air Conditioner Cooling Capacity Requirements

This relatively simple algorithm yields a rule-of-thumb estimate, measured in BTU-per-hour of the cooling capacity requirements of a central air conditioning system (a system designed to cool an entire house). Although the result will be a fairly accurate estimate for "average" climates, keep in mind that the answer is only an estimate. Plan to have a professional analysis of cooling requirements made before you purchase an air conditioning system. Here is the formula:

$$BTU/hr = (W \times 5) + (G \times 35) + (R \times 12) + (N \times 400) + 2000$$

where W = total exterior wall area of house (in square feet), G = total exterior glass area of house (in square feet), R = roof "cross section" area (in square feet), and N = number of occupants in house.

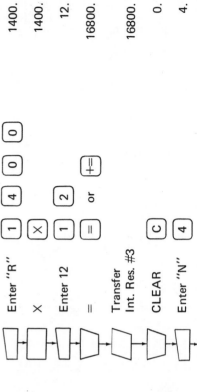

keyboard	display
Enter "R" [1] [4] [0] [0] [×]	1400.
	1400.
Enter 12 [1] [2]	12.
[=]	16800.
Transfer Int. Res. #3 [=] or [+=]	16800.
CLEAR [C]	0.
Enter "N" [4]	4.

EXAMPLE 5-8: Estimate the required cooling capacity of a central air conditioner for a house with a 1,500-sq ft external wall area, 200-sq ft exterior glass area, 1,400 sq ft roof cross section area, and four occupants. *Answer:* 34,900 BTU-per-hour.

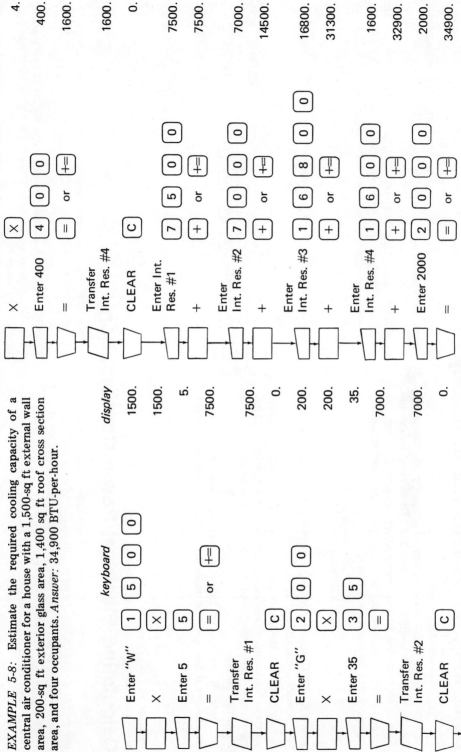

Comparing Air Conditioner Efficiency

Take your calculator with you when you go shopping for an air conditioner. It will help you compute simple "guide numbers" for the different machines you consider. These numbers can be used to compare the relative *operating efficiencies* of the various models (that is electrical power consumption per unit of cooling capacity). The formula is as follows:

$$\text{Guide Number} = \frac{B}{W}$$

where B = BTU-per-hour cooling capacity of air conditioner, and W = power consumption of air conditioner (in watts).

Try to find the make and model with the highest guide number. Operating efficiency is important, because small differences can represent savings of several dollars per year in electricity costs.

Note: If the wattage rating (power consumption) of an air conditioner is not specified on its ratings plate, use the procedure on page 82 to calculate wattage from specified voltage and current requirements.

EXAMPLE 5-9: Calculate the "guide number" for an air conditioner with a rated cooling capacity of 22,000 BTU-per-hour and a power consumption of 3500 watts. *Answer:* 6.29.

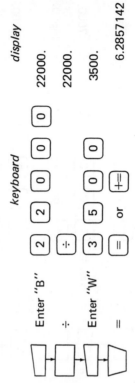

	keyboard	display
Enter "B"	2 2 0 0 0	22000.
÷	÷	22000.
Enter "W"	3 5 0 0	3500.
=	= or +÷	6.2857142

Calculating Electrical Power Consumption

This is a fundamental electrical computation that calculates the power consumption, measured in *watts*, of an appliance or device using a specified operating voltage and specified current consumption. The formula is as follows:

$$\text{Watts} = V \times I$$

for inductive device power consumption will be within 20 to 30 percent of the true value.

EXAMPLE 5-10: A toaster is rated to operate on 120 volts ac; it draws 8.2 amperes of current. What is its power consumption? *Answer:* 984 watts.

where V = specified operating voltage or line voltage (in volts), and I = specified (rated) current consumption (in amperes).

This formula yields an exact answer only when applied to direct current (dc) circuits or to those alternating current (ac) circuits which are made up of resistance elements (heating coils, incandescent light bulbs, etc.). It can be used to *estimate* the power consumption of ac circuits that contain motors, transformers, and other inductive devices. In most cases, the estimate

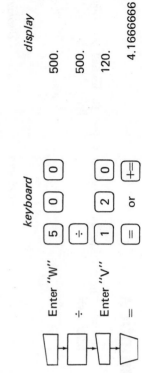

	keyboard	display
Enter "V"	1 2 0	120.
×		120.
Enter "I"	8 . 2	8.2
= or +=		984.

Calculating Electrical Appliance Current Load

Here's a simple procedure for computing the current, measured in amperes, drawn by an electric appliance, given a specific operating voltage and power consumption level. Broadly speaking, this calculation yields an exact answer only when applied to direct-current (dc) circuits or those alternating-current (ac) circuits which contain resistance elements (heating coils, incandescent light bulbs, etc.). In most cases, it will yield a reasonable estimate of the current drawn by motors, transformers, and other inductive devices. The formula:

$$\text{Current} = \frac{W}{V}$$

in which V = specified operating voltage or line voltage (in volts), and W = specified (rated) power consumption (in watts).

EXAMPLE 5-11: How much current is drawn by a 500-watt incandescent light bulb operating on 120 volts ac? *Answer:* 4.2 amperes ac.

	keyboard	display
Enter "W"	5 0 0	500.
÷		500.
Enter "V"	1 2 0	120.
= or +=		4.1666666

Calculating Electrical Energy Consumption

This simple procedure calculates the electrical energy consumption, measured in kilowatt-hours, of an electrical appliance operating for a specified period of time and consuming power at a known wattage level. The kilowatt-hour (kwh) is the standard unit of electrical energy; all household electric meters indicate total kwh consumption. The formula is as follows:

$$KWH = \frac{W \times T}{1000}$$

where T = operating time (in hours), and W = power consumption (in watts).

You can estimate the cost of running an appliance for a given period of time by multiplying the kwh consumption by the unit cost of a kwh (check with your power company for specific cost information).

EXAMPLE 5-12: How much electrical energy is consumed by a 250-watt light bulb as it operates for 15 hours? *Answer:* 3.75 kwh.

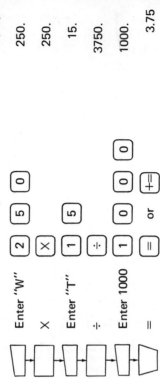

	keyboard		display
Enter "W"	[2] [5] [0]		250.
×	[×]		250.
Enter "T"	[1] [5]		15.
÷	[÷]		3750.
Enter 1000	[1] [0] [0] [0]		1000.
=	[=] or [+=]		3.75

Cutting Wheel Calculations

This pair of simple procedures can be applied to any rotating cutting tool, such as a saw blade or cutting wheel. The first formula yields the cutting speed "S" (in feet per minute) of a tool being spun at a given "RPM" (revolutions per minute); the second formula yields the "RPM" necessary to produce a required cutting speed. Here are the formulas:

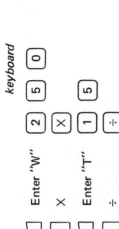

×		14400.
Enter 0.2618	[.] [2] [6] [1] [8]	0.2618
=	[=] or [+=]	3769.92

$$S = D \times RPM \times 0.2618 \qquad RPM = \frac{3.818 \times S}{D}$$

where S = cutting speed (in feet per minute), and D = tool diameter (in inches).

EXAMPLE 5-13: What is the cutting speed of an 8-inch diameter saw blade that is spinning at 1,800 revolutions per minute? Answer: 3,769.9 feet per minute.

keyboard	display
Enter "D" 8	8.
×	8.
Enter "RPM" 1 8 0 0	1800.

EXAMPLE 5-14: How fast must a 10-inch diameter grinding wheel be spun to produce a cutting speed of 4,000 feet per minute? Answer: 1,527 revolutions per minute.

keyboard	display
Enter "S" 4 0 0 0	4000.
×	4000.
Enter 3.818 3 . 8 1 8	3.818
÷	15272.
Enter "D" 1 0	10.
= or +÷	1527.2

Calculating Board-Footage of Lumber

Wood is usually sold on the basis of untrimmed dimensions, that is, the size of a board before it was planed smooth. Thus, a "one-by-eight" board actually measures about 3/4 inch thick and 7 1/4 inches wide. By definition, a *board foot*, the standard unit of wood volume, is equal to 144 cubic inches of wood.

$$\text{Board feet} = \frac{W \times T \times L}{12}$$

where W = untrimmed width of board (in inches), T = untrimmed thickness of board (in inches), L = length of board (in feet).

EXAMPLE 5-15: How many board feet of wood are contained in a piece of "two-by-eight" lumber that measures 15 feet long? Answer: 20 board-feet.

keyboard	display
Enter "W" 8	8.
×	8.

(Continued diagram)

keyboard	display
Enter "T" [2]	2.
×	
Enter "L" [1][5]	15.
÷	240.
Enter 12 [1][2]	12.
= or [+÷]	20.

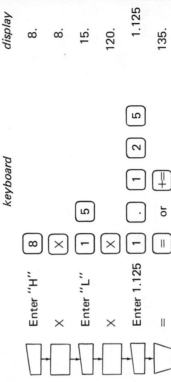

keyboard	display
Enter "H" [8]	8.
×	8.
Enter "L" [1][5]	15.
×	120.
Enter 1.125 [1][.][1][2][5]	1.125
= or [+÷]	135.

Concrete Block Estimator

This algorithm yields the number of concrete "cinder blocks" needed to build a wall of specified dimensions. It automatically takes account of the thickness of a typical layer of mortar between adjacent blocks. Here is the formula:

$$\text{Number of blocks} = H \times L \times 1.125$$

where H = height of wall (in feet), and L = length (in feet).

Note: A noninteger answer—such as 151.875—means that the wall you have described by your height and length measurements cannot be built completely out of standard size concrete blocks.

EXAMPLE 5-16: How many cinder blocks are required to build a wall measuring 8 feet high by 15 feet long? *Answer*: 135 blocks.

Concrete Calculations

The first algorithm in this pair of handy procedures estimates the number of cubic yards of concrete necessary to build a rectangular slab of given dimensions; the second algorithm calculates the individual quantities, in cubic feet, of cement, sand, and aggregate that must be combined to produce a given cubic

$$A = F_a \times Y$$

where Y = required volume of concrete (in cubic yards), C = required volume of cement (in cubic feet or bags), F_c = cement factor (from table), S = required volume of sand (in cubic feet), F_s

yardage of concrete of given formulation. For the first,

$$Y = \frac{L \times W \times T}{324}$$

where Y = volume of concrete (in cubic yards), L = length of slab (in feet), W = width (in feet), and T = thickness (in inches).

If either the L or W dimensions of the slab is not an integer multiple of feet (e.g., 6 feet, 8 feet), the inches part of the dimension must be converted into a decimal fraction of one foot by dividing it by 12. Thus, 6 feet, 8 inches becomes 6.67 feet.

There are many different formulations of concrete, each designed for a specific purpose. Each formulation has a different ratio of cement to sand to aggregate (gravel), and the respective proportions of the three constituents are specified in the "name" of the mix. For example, 1:2:3 concrete has one part cement, two parts sand, and three parts aggregate. The following procedure, and factor table, lets you compute the specific quantities of cement, sand, and aggregate necessary to produce a specific volume of concrete. By selecting the appropriate factors from the table, you "define" a specific concrete formulation for the procedure. There are three simple formulas:

$$C = F_c \times Y$$
$$S = F_s \times Y$$

= sand factor (from table), A = required volume of aggregate (in cubic feet), and F_a = aggregate factor from table.

EXAMPLE 5-17: How many cubic yards of concrete are required to build a patio slab that measures 20 feet, 6 inches long (20.5 feet), by 8 feet, 9 inches wide (8.75 feet), by 5 inches thick? *Answer:* 2.8 cubic yards.

	keyboard			display
Enter "L"	[2] [0] [.] [5]			20.5
[×]				20.5
Enter "W"	[8] [.] [7] [5]			8.75
[×]				179.375
Enter "T"	[5]			5.
[÷]				896.875
Enter 324	[3] [2] [4]			324.
[=]	or [÷=]			2.7681327

EXAMPLE 5-18: Estimate the volumes of cement, sand, and aggregate necessary to make 3 cubic yards of 1:3:4 concrete. *Answer:* 15.3 cubic feet of cement; 45.3 cubic feet of sand; 60.9 cubic feet of aggregate. *Note:* The sum of the volumes of cement, sand, and aggregate exceed the required yardage of cement because the aggregate volume includes a good deal of "open space" that will be filled by the cement and sand.)

Factor	1:1¾:2	1:2:2¾	1:2:3	1:2¾:3½	1:3:4	1:2½:3
Formulation						
F_c	8.6	7.9	6.8	5.7	5.1	6.5
F_s	14.9	15.4	13.5	14.6	15.1	14.6
F_a	17	17.3	20.3	20.3	20.3	19.4

keyboard		display
Enter "F_s" [1] [4] [.] [6]		
[=]		14.6
or [+=]		43.8
		THIS IS "S"
Enter "F_a" [2] [0] [.] [3]		
[=]		20.3
or [+=]		60.9
		THIS IS "A"

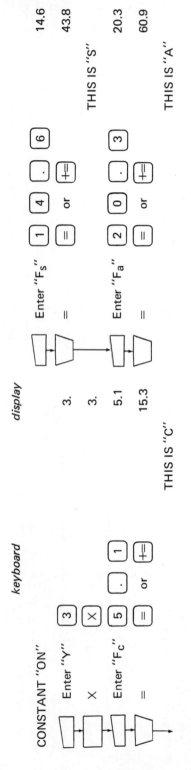

CONSTANT "ON"

keyboard		display
Enter "Y" [3] [×]		
		3.
		3.
Enter "F_c" [5] [.] [1]		
[=]		5.1
or [+=]		15.3
		THIS IS "C"

Gear, Chain, and Belt Drive Calculations

When two gears are meshed together, the speed of the driven gear is related to the speed of the driving gear (the gear connected to the powerplant) by the following formula:

$$RPM_{driven} = \frac{RPM_{driving} \times N_{driving}}{N_{driven}}$$

where N_{driven} = number of teeth of driven gear, and $N_{driving}$ = number of teeth of driving gear.

EXAMPLE 5-19: A gear with 36 teeth is driving another gear having 54 teeth. The driving gear turns at 135 revolutions per minute. What is the speed of the driven gear? *Answer*: 90 revolutions per minute.

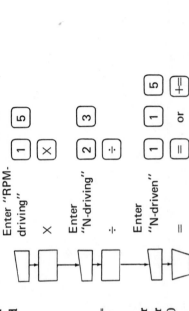

keyboard		display
Enter "RPM-driving" [1] [5] [×]		
		15.
		15.
Enter "N-driving" [2] [3] [÷]		
		23.
		345.
Enter "N-driven" [1] [1] [5]		
[=]		115.
or [+=]		3.

keyboard	display
Enter "RPM-driving" $\boxed{1}\ \boxed{3}\ \boxed{5}$	135.
$\boxed{\times}$	135.
Enter "N-driving" $\boxed{3}\ \boxed{6}$	36.
$\boxed{\div}$	4680.
Enter "N-driven" $\boxed{5}\ \boxed{4}$	54.
$\boxed{=}$ or $\boxed{+=}$	90.

When two pulleys are linked together by a drive belt, the speed of the driven pulley is related to the speed of the driving pulley by the following formula:

$$RPM_{driven} = \frac{RPM_{driving} \times D_{driving}}{D_{driven}}$$

where D_{driven} = diameter of driven pulley (in inches), and $D_{driving}$ = diameter of driving pulley (in inches).

EXAMPLE 5-21: Two pulleys are connected by a drive belt. The driving pulley is 9 inches in diameter and turns at 3,600 revolutions per minute. How fast does the 6-inch driven pulley turn? *Answer:* 5,400 revolutions per minute.

keyboard	display
Enter "RPM-driving" $\boxed{3}\ \boxed{6}\ \boxed{0}\ \boxed{0}$	3600.
$\boxed{\times}$	3600.
Enter "D-driving" $\boxed{9}$	9.
$\boxed{\div}$	32400.
Enter "D-driven" $\boxed{6}$	6.
$\boxed{=}$ or $\boxed{+=}$	5400.

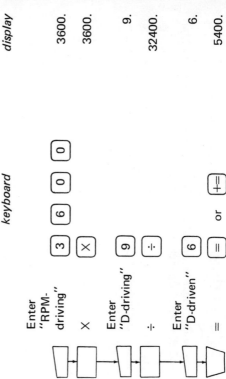

When two sprockets are linked together by a chain, the speed of the driven sprocket is related to the speed of the driving sprocket by the following formula:

$$RPM_{driven} = \frac{RPM_{driving} \times N_{driving}}{N_{driven}}$$

where N_{driven} = number of teeth on driven sprocket, and $N_{driving}$ = number of teeth on driving sprocket.

EXAMPLE 5-20: A chain drive system has a driving sprocket with 23 teeth and a driven sprocket with 115 teeth. The driving sprocket turns at 15 revolutions per minute. How fast does the driven sprocket turn? *Answer:* 3 revolutions per minute.

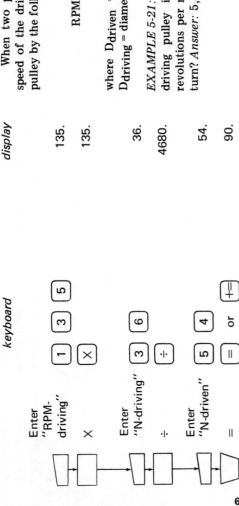

Estimating the Capacity of Liquid Storage Tanks

Be it a tropical fish tank, an oil storage tank, or a water tank, the chances are good that one of the three procedures outlined below can be used to calculate its fluid capacity (in gallons).

Rectangular tanks (Fig. 5-1):

$$C = L \times W \times D \times 0.0043$$

where C = capacity (in gallons), L = length (in inches), W = width (in inches), and D = depth (in inches).

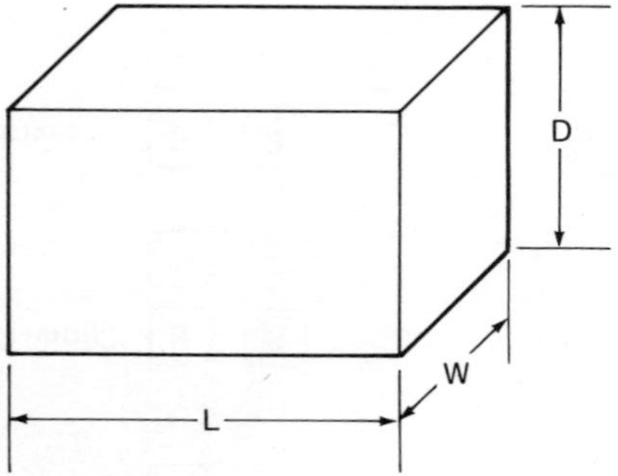

Figure 5-1

EXAMPLE 5-22: A tropical fish tank measures 36 inches long, by 12 inches wide, by 20 inches deep. Find its capacity. *Answer:* 37.2 gallons.

where C = capacity (in gallons), D = diameter of tank (in inches), and H = height (in inches).

EXAMPLE 5-23: A cylindrical water tank has a diameter of 30 inches and a height of 48 inches. What is its capacity? *Answer:* 146.9 gallons.

	keyboard			display
Enter "D"	3	0		30.
×	×			30.
=	=	or	+|=	900.
Transfer Int. Res.*				900.
CLEAR*	C			0.
Enter Int. Res.	9	0	0	900.
×	×			900.
Enter "H"	4	8		48.
×	×			43200.
Enter 0.0034	.	0	0 3 4	0.0034

$= \boxed{=}$ or $\boxed{+=}$ 146.88

*These steps may not be necessary on your calculator. They have been included to ensure that the procedure will work on a dual "=" key machine equipped for "automatic constant" operation.

Oil storage tanks (Fig. 5-3):

$$C = [(3.1416 \times R^2) + (A \times W)] \times L \times 0.0043$$

where C = capacity (in gallons), R = radius of round sections (in inches), A = spacing between round sections (in inches), W = width of tank end (in inches), and L = length (in inches).

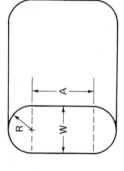

Figure 5-3

EXAMPLE 5-24: An oil storage tank is 60 inches long and has an end width of 18 inches. The radius of the round sections is 9 inches. The spacing between the round sections is 24 inches. Find its capacity. *Answer:* 177.1 gallons.

keyboard	display
Enter "L" [3][6]	36.
×	36.
Enter "W" [1][2]	12.
×	432.
Enter "D" [2][0]	20.
×	8640.
Enter 0.0043 [.][0][0][4][3]	0.0043
= or [+=]	37.152

Cylindrical tanks (Fig. 5-2):

$$C = D^2 \times H \times 0.0034$$

Figure 5-2

Single "=" key keyboard

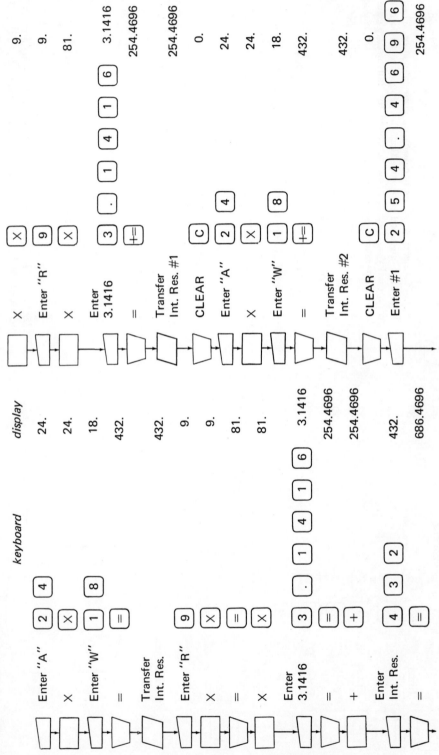

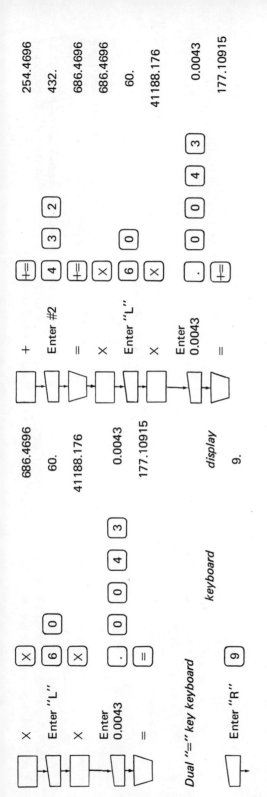

	254.4696
$\boxed{+}$ $\boxed{4}$	432.
Enter #2	686.4696
$\boxed{+}$ $\boxed{\times}$	686.4696
$\boxed{6}$ $\boxed{\times}$	60.
Enter "L"	41188.176
$\boxed{.}$ $\boxed{+}$	0.0043
Enter 0.0043	177.10915

+ ... Enter #2 ... = ... × ... Enter "L" ... × ... Enter 0.0043 ... =

$\boxed{\times}$ $\boxed{6}$ $\boxed{\times}$ $\boxed{0}$ $\boxed{0}$ $\boxed{4}$ $\boxed{3}$ 686.4696

× ... Enter "L" ... × ... Enter 0.0043 ... =

$\boxed{.}$ $\boxed{=}$ 60.

41188.176

0.0043

177.10915

Dual "=" key keyboard   *keyboard*   *display*

9.

Enter "R" $\boxed{9}$

73

6
Hobbies

Automotive Calculations

Broadly speaking, automotive calculations consist of simple procedures that use not-so-simple numbers. Consequently, your calculator makes a fine "automotive accessory," whether you are an avid road rallyer, or just a daily commuter. Here is a series of basic automotive computations that cover all aspects of automotive use and technology. The following symbols are used in many of the calculations:

T	= time (in minutes or hours)
D	= distance (in miles)
M	= velocity (in miles per hour)
RPM	= engine speed (revolutions per minute)
K	= velocity (in kilometers per hour)
MPG	= miles-per-gallon fuel consumption

1. Fuel economy—miles-per-gallon unknown:

$$MPG = \frac{D_t}{G_t}$$

where D_t = distance traveled (in miles), and G_t = gasoline consumed (in gallons).

EXAMPLE 6-1: A car travels 235 miles on 17.4 gallons of gas. Find the miles-per-gallon figure. *Answer:* 13.5 miles per gallon.

EXAMPLE 6-3: A car has a rated "fuel economy" of 17.8 miles per gallon. How many gallons of gasoline are required to propel it 375 miles? *Answer:* 21.1 gallons.

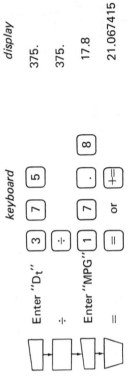

	keyboard	display
Enter "D$_t$"	3 7 5	375.
	$\div$	375.
Enter "MPG"	1 7 $.$ 8	17.8
	$=$ or $+=$	21.067415

4. Engine displacement:

$$V = 3.1416 \times B \times S \times N$$

where V = displacement (cubic inches), B = bore (inches), S = stroke (inches), and N = number of cylinders.

EXAMPLE 6-4: An eight-cylinder engine has a bore of 2.5 inches and a stroke of 3 inches. Find the total displacement. *Answer:* 188.5 cubic inches.

	keyboard	display
Enter 3.1416	3 . 1 4 1 6	3.1416
×	×	3.1416
Enter "B"	2 . 5	2.5
×	×	7.854
Enter "S"	3	3.
×	×	23.562
Enter "N"	8	8.
=	= or +=	188.496

2. Fuel economy—distance unknown:

$$D_t = MPG \times G_t$$

EXAMPLE 6-2: A car has a typical "fuel economy" of 21.2 miles per gallon. How far will it travel on 23 gallons of gasoline? *Answer: 487.6 miles.*

	keyboard	display
Enter "MPG"	2 1 . 2	21.2
×	×	21.1
Enter "G_t"	2 3	23.
=	= or +=	487.6

3. Fuel economy—gallons unknown:

$$G_t = \frac{D_t}{MPG}$$

	keyboard	display
Enter "D_t"	2 3 5	235.
÷	÷	235.
Enter "G_t"	1 7 . 4	17.4
=	= or +=	13.505747

5. Compression ratio:

$$R_c = \frac{V_c + V}{V_c}$$

where R_c = compression ratio, V_c = total clearance volume (in cubic inches), and V = total engine displacement (in cubic inches).

EXAMPLE 6-5: An engine has a displacement of 250 cubic inches and a clearance volume of 35 cubic inches. Find the compression ratio. *Answer: 8.14-to-1.*

	keyboard	display
Enter "V_c"	3 5	35.

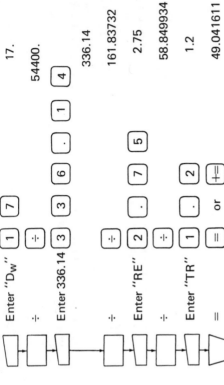

keyboard	display
+	35.
Enter "V" 2 5 0	250.
= or +=	285.
÷	285.
Enter "Vc" 3 5	35.
= or +=	8.1428571

6. Engine speed versus road speed:

$$RPM = \frac{336.14 \times M \times RE \times TR}{D_W}$$

where RPM = engine speed, M = road speed, RE = rear-end ratio, TR = transmission ratio, D_W = total diameter of wheels (in inches).

EXAMPLE 6-6: Estimate the engine speed (revolutions per minute) of a car going 60 miles per hour that has a 2.56-to-1 rear-end ratio, a 1-to-1 transmission ratio, and 18-inch diameter wheels. Answer: 2868 revolutions per minute.

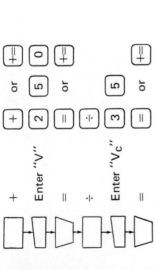

keyboard	display
Enter 336.14 3 6 . 1 4	336.14
×	336.14

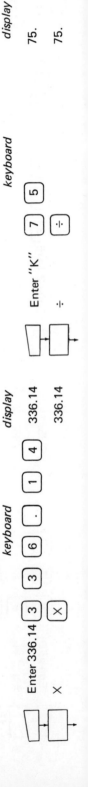

keyboard	display
Enter "Dw" 1 7	17.
÷	54400.
Enter 336.14 3 6 . 1 4	336.14
÷	161.83732
Enter "RE" 2 . 7 5	2.75
÷	58.849934
Enter "TR" 1 . 2	1.2
= or +=	49.041611

8. Kilometers per hour to miles per hour:

$$M = \frac{K}{1.60934}$$

EXAMPLE 6-8: Convert 75-kilometers per hour to miles per hour. Answer: 46.6 miles per hour.

keyboard	display
Enter "K" 7 5	75.
÷	75.

Enter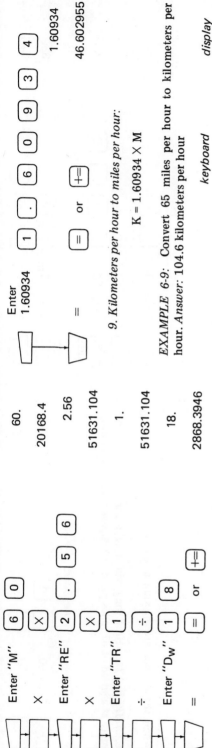
1.60934

keyboard: [1] [.] [6] [0] [9] [3] [4]   display: 1.60934

= or [+=]

46.602955

9. Kilometers per hour to miles per hour:

$$K = 1.60934 \times M$$

EXAMPLE 6-9: Convert 65 miles per hour to kilometers per hour. *Answer:* 104.6 kilometers per hour

keyboard   display

Enter
1.60934   1.60934

[1] [.] [6] [0] [9] [3] [4]   1.60934

×

Enter "M"   [6] [5]   65.

= or [+=]   104.6071

10. Time/Distance/Velocity—Distance unknown:

$$D = M \times T_h \qquad \text{or} \qquad D = \frac{M \times T_m}{60}$$

where M = road speed, T_h = time (in *hours*), and T_m = time (in *minutes*).

Enter "M"   [6] [0]   60.
×   20168.4
Enter "RE"   [2] [.] [5] [6]   2.56
×   51631.104
Enter "TR"   [1]   1.
÷   51631.104
Enter "Dw"   [1] [8]   18.
= or [+=]   2868.3946

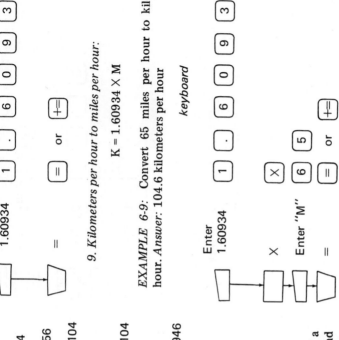

7. Road speed versus engine speed:

$$M = \frac{RPM \times D_w}{336.14 \times RE \times TR}$$

where the symbols are the same as above.

EXAMPLE 6-7: Estimate the road speed (miles per hour) of a car whose engine is turning at 3200 revolutions per minute and that has a 2.75-to-1 rear end ratio, a 1.2-to-1 transmission ratio, and 17-inch diameter wheels. *Answer:* 49 miles per hour.

keyboard   display

Enter "RPM"   [3] [2] [0] [0]   3200.
×   3200.

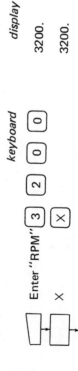

Hobbies

EXAMPLE 6-10: A car travels for 47 minutes at a velocity of 54 miles per hour. How far does it travel? *Answer:* 42.3 miles.

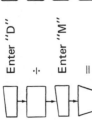

keyboard		display
Enter "M"	5 4	54.
×		54.
Enter "T_m"	4 7	47.
÷		2538.
Enter 60	6 0	60.
= or +|=		42.3

11. Time/Distance/Velocity—Time unknown:

$$T_h = \frac{D}{M} \qquad or \qquad T_m = \frac{60 \times D}{M}$$

where the symbols are the same as above.

EXAMPLE 6-11: How long will it take for a car to travel 75 miles at a speed of 37 miles per hour? *Answer:* 121.6 minutes.

keyboard		display
Enter 60	6 0	60.
×		60.
Enter "D"	7 5	75.
÷		4500.
Enter "M"	3 7	37.
= or +|=		121.62162

12. Time/Distance/Velocity—Velocity unknown:

$$M = \frac{D}{T_h} \qquad or \qquad M = \frac{60 \times D}{T_m}$$

where the symbols are the same as above.

EXAMPLE 6-12: How fast must a car travel to cover 23.5 miles in 38 minutes? *Answer:* 37.1 miles per hour

keyboard		display
Enter 60	6 0	60.
×		60.
Enter "D"	2 3 . 5	23.5
÷		1410.
Enter "T_m"	3 8	38.
= or +|=		37.105263

Estimating Electronic Photoflash Guide Number

The *guide number* of an electronic photoflash unit is usually determined by the manufacturer by photographic testing. However, the procedure outlined below can be used to estimate—with acceptable accuracy—the guide number of any flash unit that lacks a factory rating. Here is the formula:

$$GN = \sqrt{0.175 \times M \times W \times ASA}$$

where GN = guide number; M = "reflector factor" of reflector behind the flash tube—assume M = 8 for narrow-beam reflector, M = 7 for average-beam reflector, M = 6 for wide-beam reflector; W = energy of flash (in watt-seconds); and ASA = ASA "index" of film to be used.

Note: This procedure requires that a square root be calculated. Use the algorithm on page 96.

EXAMPLE 6-13: An electronic photoflash unit has an energy-per-flash of 125 watt-seconds, and a wide-beam reflector. What is its guide number for ASA 400 film? *Answer:* GN = 229.

Single and dual "=" key calculators

keyboard	display
Enter 0.175 · 1 7 5	0.175
×	0.175
Enter "M" 6	6.
×	1.05
Enter "W" 1 2 5	125.
×	131.25
Enter "ASA" 4 0 0	400.
= or +=	52500.

Use square root procedure on page 96 to calculate final answer. Guide number = 229 (to closest integer).

Photoflash Guide Number Calculations

The guide number (or "GN") of a photoflash unit—as determined for a specific type of film—is a convenient device for interrelating the *f-stop* (lens opening) and subject-to-camera distance necessary to produce a correctly exposed photograph.

By definition, the guide number equals the product of f-stop multiplied by distance. However, the formula is most useful when it is "turned inside out" to yield either the correct f-stop for a given distance or the correct distance for a given f-stop.

1. F-stop unknown:

$$f\text{-stop} = \frac{GN}{D}$$

where GN = guide number for specific film, and D = camera-to-subject distance (in *feet*).

Note: This procedure assumes that the flash unit is mounted on or near the camera and is directed at the subject.

EXAMPLE 6-14: An electronic flash unit has a guide number of 65 for ASA 80 film. What is the correct f-stop for a subject 12 feet away from the camera? *Answer*: f/5.6 (closest f-stop to answer of 5.42).

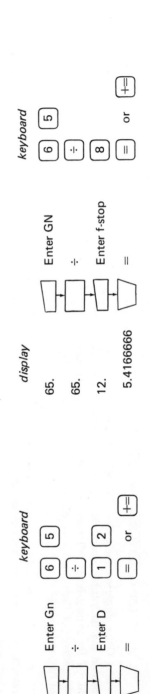

	keyboard	display
Enter Gn	6 5	65.
÷	÷	65.
Enter D	1 2	12.
	= or +=	5.4166666

2. Distance unknown:

$$D = \frac{GN}{f\text{-stop}}$$

where the symbols are the same as defined above.

Note: This procedure assumes that the flash unit is mounted on or near the camera and is directed at the subject.

EXAMPLE 6-15: The same flash unit described above will be used to illuminate a subject to make a photograph on ASA 80 film. The photographer wishes to set his lens opening to f/8. What should the camera-to-subject distance be? *Answer*: Approximately 8 feet.

	keyboard	display
Enter GN	6 5	65.
÷	÷	65.
Enter f-stop	8	8.
	= or +=	8.125

Electronic Circuit Calculations

Here is a collection of fundamental—and exceptionally useful—calculations for electronic circuits containing *passive* components (resistors, capacitors, and inductors). Unless otherwise noted, all of the formulas use the following set of symbols:

EXAMPLE 6-17: How much current will flow through a 1,000,000 ohm resistor that is connected across a voltage of 135 volts? *Answer*: 0.00135 amperes (or 0.13 milliamperes)

R = resistance (in *ohms*)
L = inductance (in *henrys*)
C = capacitance (in *farads*)
I = current (in *amperes*)
E = voltage (in *volts*)
W = power (in *watts*)
λ = wavelength (in *meters*)
f = frequency (in *Hertz*)

	keyboard	display
Enter E	[1] [3] [5]	135.
÷		135.
Enter R	[1] [0] [0] [0] [0] [0] [0]	1000000.
= or [+=]		0.000135

1. Ohm's Law—voltage unknown:

$$E = I \times R$$

EXAMPLE 6-16: **What is the voltage produced across a resistance of 1200 ohms by a current of 0.36 amperes flowing through it?** *Answer:* **432 volts.**

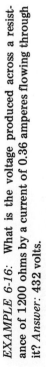
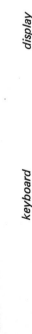

	keyboard	display
Enter I	[0] [.] [3] [6]	0.36
×		0.36
Enter R	[1] [2] [0] [0]	1200.
= or [+=]		432.

2. Ohm's Law—current unknown:

$$I = \frac{E}{R}$$

3. Ohm's Law—resistance unknown:

$$R = \frac{E}{I}$$

EXAMPLE 6-18: **What resistance should be connected across a voltage of 50 volts to establish a current flow of 0.15 amperes?** *Answer:* **333.33 ohms.**

	keyboard	display
Enter E	[5] [0]	50.
÷		50.
Enter I	[.] [1] [5]	0.15
= or [+=]		333.33333

4. DC Power—voltage and current known:

$$W = E \times I$$

EXAMPLE 6-19: How much power is being supplied by a dc power supply that has a 12-volt output voltage and 4.2-ampere output current? *Answer:* 50.4 watts.

keyboard		display
Enter E	1 2	12.
×		12.
Enter I	4 . 2	4.2
= or +=		50.4

Single "=" key calculator

	keyboard	display
Enter "I"	2	2.
×		2.
×		4.
Enter "R"	8	8.
=		32.

Dual "=" key calculator

	keyboard	display
Enter I	2	2.
×		2.
Enter I	2	2.
×		4.
Enter R	8	8.
=		32.

5. DC Power—voltage and resistance known:

$$W = \frac{E^2}{R}$$

EXAMPLE 6-20: How much power is being dissipated by a 500-ohm resistor that is connected across a 24-volt power supply? *Answer:* 1.15 watts.

Single "=" key calculator

	keyboard	display
Enter "E"	2 4	24.

7. Two resistors (or inductors) in parallel (Fig. 6-1):

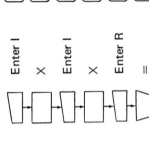

$$R = \frac{R_1 \times R_2}{R_1 + R_2}$$

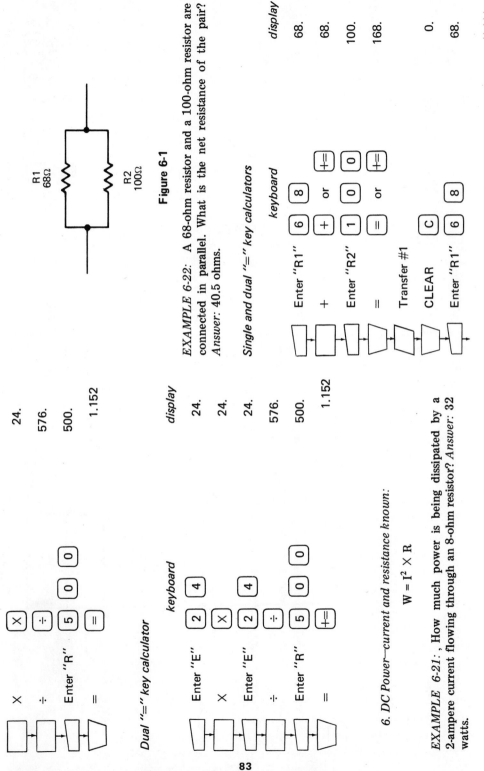

R1 68Ω **R2 100Ω**

Figure 6-1

EXAMPLE 6-22: A 68-ohm resistor and a 100-ohm resistor are connected in parallel. What is the net resistance of the pair? *Answer:* 40.5 ohms.

Single and dual "=" key calculators

	keyboard		display
Enter "R1"	[6] [8]		68.
+	[+] or [+=]		68.
Enter "R2"	[1] [0] [0]		100.
=	[=] or [+=]		168.
Transfer #1			
CLEAR	[C]		0.
Enter "R1"	[6] [8]		68.

× [×]
÷ [÷]
Enter "R" [5] [0] [0]
= [=]

display: 24. 576. 500. 1.152

Dual "=" key calculator

	keyboard		display
Enter "E"	[2] [4]		24.
×	[×]		24.
Enter "E"	[2] [4]		24.
÷	[÷]		576.
Enter "R"	[5] [0] [0]		500.
=	[+=]		1.152

6. DC Power—current and resistance known:

$$W = I^2 \times R$$

EXAMPLE 6-21: How much power is being dissipated by a 2-ampere current flowing through an 8-ohm resistor? *Answer:* 32 watts.

83

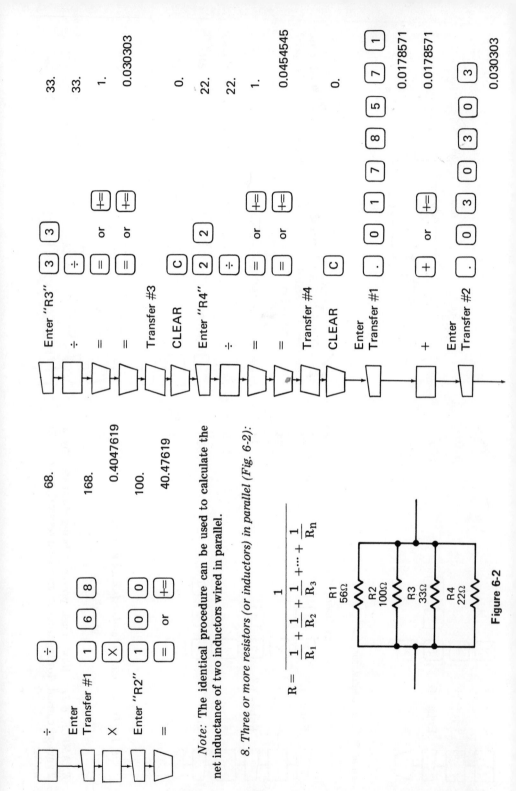

Enter "R3" | 3 | 3 |
÷
=   or   =
=   or   =
Transfer #3
CLEAR | C |
Enter "R4" | 2 | 2 |
÷
=   or   =
=   or   =
Transfer #4
CLEAR | C |
Enter Transfer #1 | . | 0 | 1 | 7 | 8 | 5 | 7 | 1 |
+   or   =
Enter Transfer #2 | . | 0 | 3 | 0 | 3 | 0 | 3 |

33.
33.
1.
0.030303
0.
22.
22.
1.
0.0454545
0.
0.0178571
0.0178571
0.030303

÷
Enter Transfer #1 | 1 | 6 | 8 |
×
Enter "R2" | 1 | 0 | 0 |
=   or   =

68.
168.
0.4047619
100.
40.47619

Note: The identical procedure can be used to calculate the net inductance of two inductors wired in parallel.

8. *Three or more resistors (or inductors) in parallel (Fig. 6-2):*

$$R = \frac{1}{\dfrac{1}{R_1} + \dfrac{1}{R_2} + \dfrac{1}{R_3} + \cdots + \dfrac{1}{R_n}}$$

R1 56Ω   R2 100Ω   R3 33Ω   R4 22Ω

Figure 6-2

EXAMPLE 6-23: A 56-ohm resistor, a 100-ohm resistor, a 33-ohm resistor, and a 22-ohm resistor are wired in parallel. What is the net resistance? *Answer*: 9.7 ohms.

Single or dual "=" key calculators

	keyboard		display
CONSTANT ON			
Enter "R"	5 6		56.
÷	=	or ＝	56.
=	=	or ＝	1.
=			0.0178571
Transfer #1			
CLEAR	C		0.
Enter "R2"	1 0 0		100.
÷	=	or ＝	100.
=	=	or ＝	1.
=			0.01
Transfer #2			
CLEAR	C		0.

	keyboard		display
+	+	or ＋	0.0481601
	0 .	or 0 1	0.01
Enter Transfer #3	＋		
+	+	or ＋	0.0581601
Enter Transfer #4			
	0 .	or 0 4 5	0.0454545
	5	or ＝	0.1036146
	＝	÷ 4 5	0.1036146
	=	=	1.
	＝	=	9.6511495

9. *Two or more resistors (or inductors) in series (Fig. 6-3)*:

$$R = R_1 + R_2 + R_3 + \ldots + R_n$$

Note: The identical procedure can be used to calculate the net inductance of three or more inductors wired in parallel.

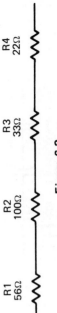

R1 56Ω   R2 100Ω   R3 33Ω   R4 22Ω

Figure 6-3

C1 2 mfd   C2 1 mfd   C3 3.5 mfd

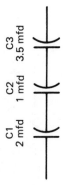

Figure 6-5

EXAMPLE: A 0.002-farad capacitor, a 0.001-farad capacitor, and a 0.0035-farad capacitor are connected in series. What is the net capacitance? *Answer*: 0.00056 farad.

12. Two or more capacitors in parallel (Fig. 6-6):

$$C = C_1 + C_2 + C_3 + \ldots + C_4$$

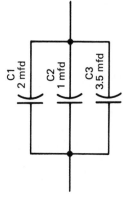

C1 2 mfd

C2 1 mfd

C3 3.5 mfd

Figure 6-6

EXAMPLE: A 0.002-farad capacitor, a 0.001-farad capacitor, and a 0.0035-farad capacitor are connected in parallel. What is the net capacitance? *Answer*: 0.0065 farad.

13. Inductive reactance:

$$X_L = f \times L \times 6.2832$$

EXAMPLE 6-24: A 56-ohm resistor, a 100-ohm resistor, a 33-ohm resistor, and a 22-ohm resistor are wired in series. What is the net resistance? *Answer*: 211 ohms.

Single and dual "=" key calculator

keyboard				display
Enter R1	5	6		56
+			or $+=$	56
Enter R2	1	0	0	100
+			or $+=$	156
Enter R3	3	3		33
+			or $+=$	189
Enter R4	2	2		22
=			or $+=$	211

Note: The identical procedure can be used to calculate the net inductance of two or more inductors in series.

CAPACITOR CALCULATIONS

The three procedures that follow calculate the net capacitance of series and parallel combinations of two or more capacitors. Although we show formulas and diagrams, we do not present algorithms or displays since the procedures are identical to the resistor calculations presented above:

where X_L = inductive reactance (in *ohms*), f = frequency, and L = inductance.

EXAMPLE 6-25: What is the reactance of a 2.2-millihenry inductance (0.0022 henry) at a frequency of 400 Hz? Answer: 5.5 ohms.

Single or dual "=" key calculators

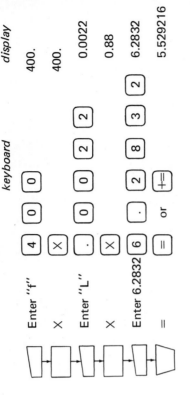

	keyboard	display
Enter "f"	4 0 0	400.
×		400.
Enter "L"	. 0 0 2 2	0.0022
×		0.88
Enter 6.2832	6 . 2 8 3 2	6.2832
	= or +=	
	=	5.529216

14. Capacitive reactance:

$$X_c = \frac{1}{6.2832 \times f \times C}$$

where X_c = capacitive reactance (in *ohms*), f = frequency, and C = capacitance.

EXAMPLE 6-26: What is the reactance of a 5000-microfarad capacitor at a frequency of 60 Hz? Answer: 0.53 ohms.

Hobbies

Two capacitors in series—Use procedure for *two resistors in parallel*.

Three or more capacitors in series—Use procedure for *three or more resistors in parallel*.

Two or more capacitors in parallel—Use procedure for *two or more resistors in series*.

10. Two capacitors in series (Fig. 6-4):

$$C = \frac{C_1 \times C_2}{C_1 + C_2}$$

C1   C2
0.1 µfd   0.22 µfd

Figure 6-4

EXAMPLE: A 0.1-microfarad (.0000001-farad) capacitor and a 0.22-microfarad (0.00000022-farad) capacitor are connected in series. What is the net capacitance? Answer: 0.069 microfarad.

Note: This calculation must be performed in microfarad units to allow entry of the capacitance values on an eight-digit calculator. As a rule of thumb, answers will be correct as long as you are consistent in your use of units throughout the computation.

11. Three or more capacitors in series (Fig. 6-5):

$$C = \frac{1}{\dfrac{1}{C_1} + \dfrac{1}{C_2} + \dfrac{1}{C_3} + \cdots + \dfrac{1}{C_n}}$$

16. Resonant circuit—inductance unknown:

$$L = \frac{1}{39.4786 \times f^2 \times C}$$

EXAMPLE 6-28: A circuit is to have a resonant frequency of 159 Hz. It will use a 0.001-farad capacitor. What should the inductance be? *Answer:* 0.001 henry.

If f is expressed in megaHertz and C is expressed in microfarads, the answer will be in units of microhenries.

	keyboard	display
Enter "f"	[1] [5] [9]	159.
×	or [+=]	159.
=		25281.
Transfer "f²"		
CLEAR	[C]	0.
Enter 1	[1]	1.
÷	[÷]	1.
Enter 39.4786	[3] [9] [.] [4] [7] [8] [6]	39.4786
÷	[÷]	0.0253301

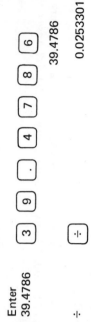

Single or dual "=" key calculator

	keyboard	display
Enter 1	[1]	1.
÷	[÷]	1.
Enter 6.2832	[6] [.] [2] [8] [3] [2]	6.2832
÷	[÷]	0.1591545
Enter "f"	[6] [0]	60.
÷	[÷]	0.0026525
Enter "C"	[.] [0] [0] [5]	0.005
=	or [+=]	0.5305

15. Resonant frequency:

$$f_r = \frac{1}{6.2832\sqrt{L \times C}}$$

where f_r = resonant frequency.

EXAMPLE 6-27: What is the resonant frequency of a tuned circuit consisting of a 0.001-farad capacitor and 0.001-henry inductor in parallel? *Answer:* 159 Hz.

If L and C are expressed in microfarads and microhenries, the resulting frequency will be in units of megaHertz (millions of

Hertz). *Note*: This procedure requires that a square root be taken. Use the algorithm on page 96.

Single or dual "=" key calculator

keyboard		display
Enter "L"	[.] [0] [0] [1]	0.001
×	[×]	0.001
Enter "C"	[.] [0] [0] [1]	0.001
=	[=] or [+=]	0.000001
Transfer		
CLEAR	[C]	0.

Use the square root procedure on page 96 to calculate the square root of the transfer = 0.001

keyboard		display
Enter 1	[1]	1.
÷	[÷]	1.
Enter Square Root	[.] [0] [0] [1]	0.001
÷	[÷]	1000.
Enter 6.2832	[6] [.] [2] [8] [3] [2]	6.2832
=	[=] or [+=]	159.15457

keyboard		display
Enter "f²"	[2] [5] [2] [8] [1]	25281.
÷	[÷]	.000001
Enter "C"	[.] [0] [0] [1]	0.001
=	[=] or [+=]	0.001

17. Resonant circuit–capacitance unknown:

$$C = \frac{1}{39.4786 \times f^2 \times L}$$

EXAMPLE: A circuit is to have a resonant frequency of 159 Hz. It will use a 0.001-henry inductor. What should the capacitance be? *Answer*: 0.001 farad. This example is identical to the previous example, with C exchanged for L throughout.

18. Converting frequency into wavelength (frequency in megaHertz):

$$\lambda = \frac{299.706}{f_m}$$

where λ = wavelength, and f_m = frequency (in megaHertz).

EXAMPLE 6-29: What is the wavelength of a 2.2-megaHertz radio wave? *Answer*: 136.23 meters.

keyboard		display
Enter 229.706	[2] [2] [9] [.] [7] [0] [6]	229.706

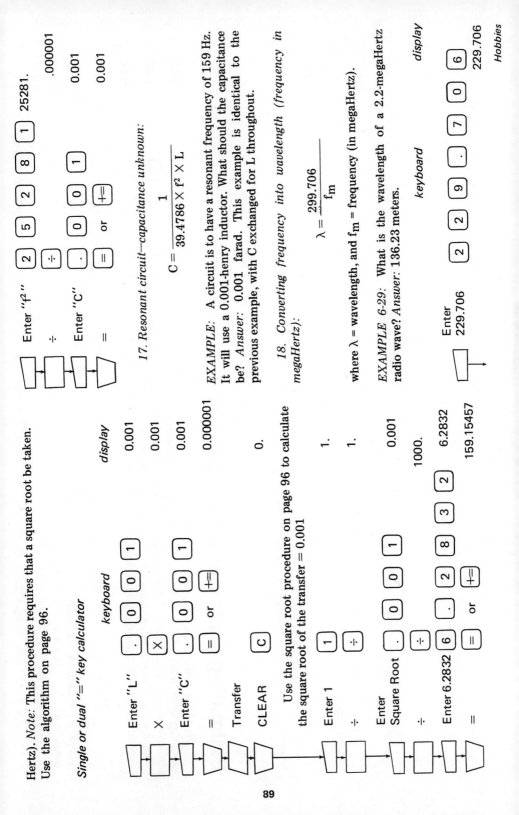

19. Converting wavelength into frequency (frequency in megaHertz):

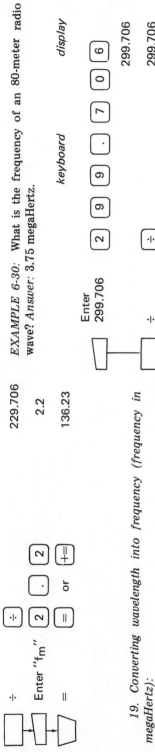

keyboard	display
÷	229.706
Enter "f_m": 2 . 2	2.2
= or +=	136.23

$$f_m = \frac{299.706}{\lambda}$$

where f_m = frequency (in megaHertz), and λ = wavelength.

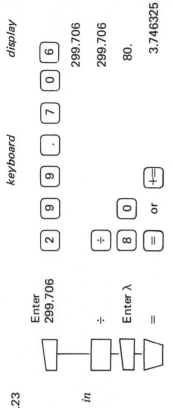

EXAMPLE 6-30: What is the frequency of an 80-meter radio wave? *Answer:* 3.75 megaHertz.

keyboard	display
2 9 9 . 7 0 6	
Enter 299.706	299.706
÷	299.706
Enter λ: 8 0	80.
= or +=	3.746325

Estimating the Travel Time of a Bullet

Here's a calculation that will be of special interest to shooting-sport hobbyists. It estimates the travel time—measured in *seconds*—of a bullet traversing a known distance when the velocities at either end are known. The formula takes into account the continuous decrease in bullet velocity as it travels:

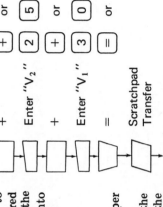

keyboard	display
+ or +=	2500.
Enter "V_2": 2 5 0 0	2500.
+ or +=	5000.
Enter "V_1": 3 0 0 0	3000.
= or +=	8000.
Scratchpad Transfer	

$$\text{Travel time (in seconds)} = \frac{3 \times D}{(2 \times V_2) + V_1}$$

where D = distance (in feet), V_1 = initial velocity (feet per second), and V_2 = final velocity (feet per second).

In most cases, the starting point will be the muzzle of the firearm (V_1 = muzzle velocity) and the end point will be the target (D = distance to target; V_2 = bullet velocity at target distance). Bullet velocities at various ranges are published by ammunition makers.

EXAMPLE 6-31: A rifle bullet has a muzzle velocity of 3000 feet per second and a 100-yard velocity of 2,500 feet per second. Estimate its travel time across a 100-yard distance (a distance of 300 feet). *Answer*: 0.11 seconds.

keyboard		display
Enter "V_2"	[2][5][0][0]	2500.
CLEAR	[C]	0.
Enter 3	[3]	3.
×	[×]	3.
Enter "D"	[3][0][0]	300.
÷	[÷]	900.
Enter Transfer	[8][0][0][0] or [÷=]	8000.
=	[=]	0.1125

Estimating Bullet Trajectory Height

This simple procedure estimates the height of the trajectory traveled by a bullet from firearm to target. Trajectory height is an important characteristic for judging the "flat-shooting" qualities of a bullet/cartridge combination. Here is the formula:

$$\text{Height (in inches)} = T^2 \times 48$$

where T = travel time of bullet (in seconds).

This formula provides a surprisingly accurate estimate of trajectory height—typically within 10 percent of the true height.

In most cases, the error is on the high side; the true trajectory is a bit lower than the estimate. *Note*: the travel time ("T") used in this calculation must be computed using the procedure in the previous section ("Estimating the Travel Time of a Bullet").

EXAMPLE: 6-32: What is the estimated trajectory height of a bullet that travels 200 yards from firearm to target in 0.17 seconds? *Answer*: 1.4 inches.

Single "=" key keyboard and dual "=" key keyboard without "automatic constant"

keyboard		display
Enter "T"	. 1 7	0.17
×		0.17
= or +|=		0.0289
×		0.0289
Enter 48	4 8	48.
= or +|=		1.3872

Dual "=" key keyboard with "automatic constant"

keyboard		display
Enter "T"	. 1 7	0.17
×		0.17
Enter "T"	. 1 7	0.17
×		0.0289
Enter 48	4 8	48.
+|=		1.3872

92

er 8 raised to the third power—written in mathematics

Mathematics

Converting to Decimal Fractions

A decimal fraction is simply a number less than one expressed in decimal form. For example, the decimal equivalent of 1/2 is 0.5. Generally speaking, you must always convert a conventional fraction to its decimal equivalent in order to use it in a calculation.

Percentages, too, can be expressed as decimal fractions. Six percent, for example, is merely a shorthand way of writing 6/100, which is equivalent to 0.06. Most of the financial calculations in this book require that the interest rate—most often stated as a percentage—be converted to a decimal fraction.

Converting a conventional fraction to a decimal fraction is easy. Just perform the indicated division operation. Here's the general formula and algorithm:

$$D = \frac{A}{B}$$

where D = decimal equivalent, A = numerator of conventional fraction, and B = denominator of conventional fraction.

EXAMPLE 7-1: Convert 5/16 to its decimal equivalent. *Answer:* 0.3125.

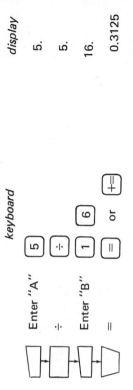

keyboard	display
Enter "A" [5]	5.
[÷]	5.
Enter "B" [1] [6]	16.
[=] or [+=]	0.3125

Percentages are just as easily converted using the following general formula and algorithm:

$$D = \frac{P}{100}$$

where P = percentage.

EXAMPLE 7-2: Convert 73 percent to a decimal fraction. *Answer:* 0.73.

keyboard		display
Enter "p" 7 3 ÷ 		73.
		73.
Enter 100 1 0 0 = or +=		100.
		0.73

Finding the Reciprocal of a Number . . . a Fast Method

By definition, the reciprocal of a given number is 1 divided by the number. Thus, the reciprocal of 8 is 1/8, or 0.125, and the reciprocal of 2.5 is 1/2.5, or 0.4.

Although you can compute a reciprocal by performing the indicated division operation, there is a faster method if your calculator is equipped with the "constant division" feature (either switch-controlled or "automatic"). The procedure can be summed up in three words: "Divide—equals—equals."

Incidentally, the reciprocal of a number less than 1 is always greater than 1, a fact that many people find confusing the first time they encounter it. Prove the point by calculating the reciprocal of 0.9999999 (the "closest" number to 1 that can be entered on an 8-digit calculator). The answer is 1.0000001.

EXAMPLE 7-3: Find the reciprocal of 16. *Answer:* 0.0625.

keyboard		display
CONSTANT "ON"		
Enter Number 1 6 		0.
÷		16.
=		16.
= or +=		1.
= or +=		0.0625

Raising a Number to a Power

Here is a procedure that is useful in its own right and also an integral part of many valuable financial calculations. Simply stated, raising a number to a power means multiplying the number by itself the specified number of times. For example, the ...

The procedure is identical for a noninteger number.

EXAMPLE 7-5: Raise 1.06 to the fifth power (1.06^5), a calculation similar to the kind found in many financial problems. *Answer:* (rounded to three decimal places): 1.338.

94

notation as 8^3—is equal to $8 \times 8 \times 8$, or 512. Similarly, 5 raised to the sixth power—written 5^6—is equal to 15,625 ($5 \times 5 \times 5 \times 5 \times 5 \times 5$), while 1.7 raised to the fourth power (or 1.7^4) equals 8.3521 ($1.7 \times 1.7 \times 1.7 \times 1.7$).

If your calculator is equipped with a "constant multiplication" feature—either switch operated or "automatic"—you can raise numbers to a power easily and quickly, literally at the touch of the "=" or "+=" key. Here's how:

1. Switch on the "constant multiplication" feature (if not an "automatic" machine).

2. Enter the number to be raised.

3. Press the "=" or "+=" key P − 1 times, where P is the required power.

keyboard		display
Enter 1.06	[1] [.] [0] [6]	1.06
[×]		1.06
[=] or [+=]		1.1236
[=] or [+=]		1.191016
[=] or [+=]		1.2624769
[=] or [+=]		1.3382255

Because many financial computations require that numbers be raised to large powers (often over 100!), it is impractical to illustrate the algorithms with complete flow charts. And so, we've used a six-sided shape to denote the operation whenever the power is greater than three. You will find the six-sided block in most of the financial procedures.

Note: If your calculator is *not* equipped for "constant multiplication," you must perform the P − 1 multiplications manually.

EXAMPLE 7-6: Raise 3 to the fourth power (3^4) manually. *Answer:* 81.

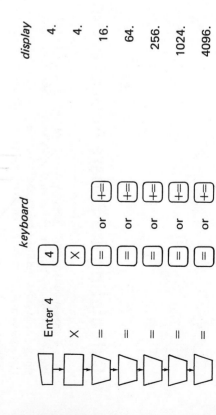

keyboard		display
Enter 3	[3]	3.
[×]		3.

Mathematics

EXAMPLE 7-4: Raise the number 4 to the sixth power (4^6). (Note that the "=" or "+=" key is pressed *five* times because P − 1 equals five.) *Answer:* 4096.

keyboard		display
Enter 4	[4]	
[×]		4.
[=] or [+=]		4.
[=] or [+=]		16.
[=] or [+=]		64.
[=] or [+=]		256.
[=] or [+=]		1024.
[=] or [+=]		4096.

Enter 3   3.
×
Enter 3   9.
            3.

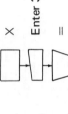

            ×   27.
Enter 3   3.
=   81.

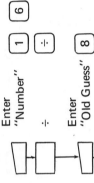

× 3
3 = or ±

Calculating the Square Root of a Number

Even though your four-function calculator is not equipped with a special square-root "key," you can use it to compute the square root of any number between 0 and about 66,666,666. The simple procedure outlined below starts with a guess, then refines the guesswork to produce an accurate result. Here's the basic formula:

$$\text{Next Guess} = \frac{\left(\dfrac{\text{Number}}{\text{Old Guess}}\right) + \text{Old Guess}}{2}$$

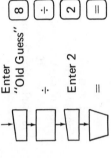

Enter "Old Guess"   8.
÷   10.
Enter 2   2.
=   5.

                This is "Next Guess"

The first step in finding a square root is to take a guess. Look carefully at the number in question, and estimate its square root. If you haven't a clue, use one-half of the number as your guess.

Now "plug" your guess into the formula (it's labeled "Old Guess" in the equation). The answer you'll come up with is called "Next Guess." Can you guess why? That's right. It goes back into the formula.

Take the answer and plug *it* into the equation. Now, of course, it is considered the "Old Guess," used to produce a fresh "Next Guess." What happens now? You guessed it! The new answer gets plugged into the formula.

When do you stop? In most cases (especially if your first guess was somewhere close to the square root), three or four

Dual "=" key keyboard

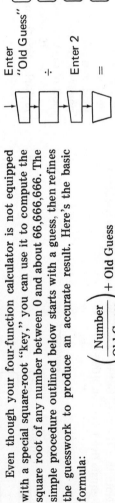

            keyboard   display
Enter "Number"   1 6   16.
÷   ÷
                             16.
Enter "Old Guess" 8   8.

times "around the loop" will yield an accurate answer. Actually, the procedure itself will tell you exactly when to stop: When the "Next Guess" is almost, or exactly, equal to the "Old Guess," you have arrived.

Note: In this procedure, it is important that you do not round-off any of the "intermediate results" ("Next Guesses") that pop up along the way). Many of the "Next Guess" answers will fill up all eight digits of the display (especially when the square root is fractional). Be sure you work accurately when you read out and re-enter scratchpad transfers. At any time during the series of calculations you can test the closeness of a "Next Guess" answer to the actual square root by multiplying it by itself.

EXAMPLE 7-7: Calculate the square root of 16 (Use 8 as the first guess). *Answer:* 4. *Note:* Each of the algorithms that follow—one for each type of keyboard configuration—illustrates a single "trip around the loop" (or, a single "iteration"). The table that follows the algorithms lists "Next Guesses" yielded by several additional trips.

Single "=" key keyboard

=	⊞	2.
Scratchpad Transfer		0.
CLEAR	C	2.
Enter Transfer	2	2.
+	⊞	8.
Enter "Old Guess"	8	10.
=	⊞	10.
÷	÷	2.
Enter 2	2	5.
=	⊞	

This is "Next Guess"

Trip	Old Guess	Next Guess
1	8	5
2	5	4.1
3	4.1	4.0012195
4	4.0012195	4.0000001
5	4.0000001	4

Single "=" key keyboard

	display	keyboard
Enter "Number"	16.	1 6
÷	16.	÷
Enter "Old Guess"	8.	8
+	2.	+

97

Mathematics

8
Fun Calculations

"Magic" Age and Number Game

There's really nothing magical about this time-worn mathematical trick. It only seems that you are guessing the participant's age and a random number (from 0 to 99) that he has selected. If you think the procedure through, you will find that the "victim" has provided the answers himself, with the long series of meaningless calculations merely serving as numerical camouflage.

For best effect, let the participant perform the first six steps of the procedure himself, using your calculator. Then, you can complete the final—secret—calculation in your head. Tell the person to do the following:

1. Multiply his age by 4, then
2. Add 14 to the answer, then
3. Multiply the sum by 25, then
4. Add any random number between 0 and 99 to the answer, then
5. Subtract 365 from the sum, and then
6. Tell you his final answer.

Now, you add 15 to the number he has given you—and look carefully. The final sum will be a three-or four-digit number. The last two digits are the participant's random number (single-digit random numbers will be preceded by a zero; 05, for example), while the first digit(s) is (are) his age.

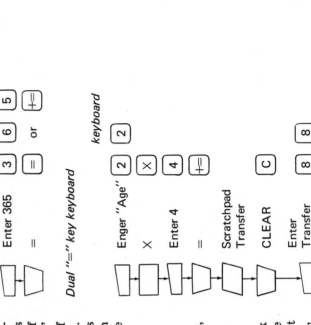

	keyboard	display
Enter 365	[3] [6] [5]	365.
=	[=] or [+=]	2260.

Dual "=" key keyboard

	keyboard	display
Enter "Age"	[2] [2]	22.
×	[×]	22.
Enter 4	[4]	4.
=	[+=]	88.
Scratchpad Transfer		
CLEAR	[C]	0.
Enter Transfer	[8] [8]	88.

EXAMPLE 8-1: Play the game with a victim who is 22 years old and who chooses 75 as his random number. *Answer:* The algorithms below yield answers of 2260. When you mentally add 15, the final answer is 2275.

Single "=" key keyboard

keyboard		display
Enter "Age"	2 2	22.
×	×	22.
Enter 4	4	4.
+	+	88.
Enter 14	1 4	14.
×	×	102.
Enter 25	2 5	25.
+	+	2550.
Enter "Random Number"	7 5	75.
−	−	2625.
		2260.

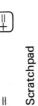

---

		display
+		88.
Enter 14	1 4	14.
=		102.
×	×	102.
Enter 25	2 5	25.
=		2550.
Scratchpad Transfer		0.
CLEAR	C	2550.
Enter Transfer	2 5	2550.
+		75.
Enter "Random Number"	7 5	2625.
+		365.
Enter 365	3 6 5	2260.
−		

Estimating the Temperature-Humidity Index (THI)

The temperature-humidity index (THI) estimates the degree of discomfort that will be felt on a hot and/or humid day. For this reason, it is often called the "discomfort index." As a rule of thumb, about 10 percent of the population is uncomfortable when the THI hits 70; about 50 percent become unhappy when the THI reaches 75; nearly everyone is miserable when the THI shoots above 80.

Usually, the THI is calculated using the following formula:

$$THI = 0.4 \times (Tw + Td) + 15$$

where Tw is the "wet-bulb temperature" and Td is the "dry-bulb temperature," both in degrees Fahrenheit. The wet-bulb temperature is measured on a special thermometer that is equipped with a water-soaked wick on its bulb.

Here, we use a somewhat simpler formula to estimate THI given the known air temperature and relative humidity:

$$THI = (0.8 \times T) + 15 - A$$

where T = air temperature (degrees F), and A = factor from the table below.

Relative Humidity	A
95% or higher	0
90% to 94%	2
80% to 89%	4
70% to 79%	6
60% to 69%	10
Less than 60%	14

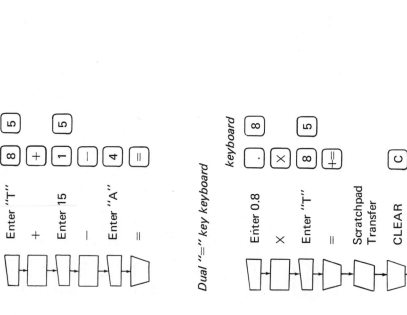

100

EXAMPLE 8-2: Estimate the THI when the temperature is 85° F and the relative humidity is 80 percent. *Answer:* THI = 79.

Single "=" key keyboard

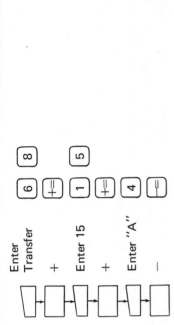

keyboard		display
Enter 0.8	. 8	0.8
×	×	0.8

Enter Transfer	6 8	68.
+	+⫞	68.
Enter 15	1 5	15.
+	+⫞	83.
Enter "A"	4	4.
−	⫞	79.

Alcohol Content of Beverages

By Federal Government definition, a "proof spirit" is an alcoholic liquor that contains 50-percent ethyl alcohol by volume. This is popularly called "100-proof" liquor. Beverages containing a smaller percentage of alcohol will have lower proof numbers: liquors with higher percentages have higher proof numbers. This procedure computes the alcohol content—measured in fluid ounces—of a specific quantity of whiskey or liquor of known proof. Here is the formula:

$$\text{Ounces of alcohol} = \frac{P \times O}{200}$$

where P = proof of beverage, and O = ounces of beverage (in fluid ounces).

Once you have calculated the liquid volume of alcohol in a given quantity of beverage, you can compute the alcohol's weight (in ounces) by multiplying your answer by 0.791.

EXAMPLE 8-3: What is the alcohol content of a pint (16 fluid ounces) of 86-proof Scotch whiskey? *Answer:* 6.9-fluid ounces.

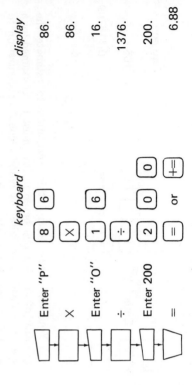

keyboard		display
Enter "P"	8 6	86.
×	×	86.
Enter "O"	1 6	16.
÷	÷	1376.
Enter 200	2 0 0	200.
=	= or +⫞	6.88

Fun Calculations

101

"Tipsiness" Estimator

Blood alcohol concentration—the percentage concentration of alcohol in the blood—is a universally accepted measure of tipsiness. Many motor vehicle "drunk driving" laws specify a maximum acceptable blood alcohol concentration. This procedure *estimates* the blood alcohol concentration, measured in percent, of an individual who has consumed a given quantity of alcoholic beverages during a one-hour period. The formula is as follows:

$$C = \frac{O \times P \times 0.037}{W}$$

where C = blood alcohol concentration (percent), W = body weight of drinker (in pounds), O = ounces of beverage consumed (fluid ounces), and P = proof of alcoholic beverage.

This formula, though based on sound physiological principles, should be used only as a rule-of-thumb guide to tipsiness. Alcohol affects different people differently. Generally speaking, blood alcohol concentrations in the range of 0.01 to 0.1 percent produce the classic tipsiness symptoms: removal of inhibitions, loss of self-control, weakening of will power, development of euphoria (feeling of well-being), etc. Higher percentages cause slurred speech, loss of skill, disturbance of equilibrium, etc. Percentages over 0.40 percent can sometimes cause death.

102

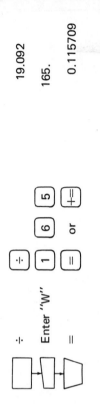

÷	19.092
÷	165.
Enter "W"	1 6 5
= or +=	0.115709

You can easily reverse this calculation to estimate the quantity of an alcoholic beverage that must be consumed by a specific individual to raise his blood alcohol concentration to some given percentage. (Here again, the calculation assumes that the beverage is being consumed during a one-hour period.) The formula is as follows:

$$O = \frac{C \times W \times 27}{P}$$

EXAMPLE 8-5: Estimate the number of ounces of 100-proof liquor that can be consumed by a 180-pound person who wishes to keep his blood alcohol concentration below 0.05 percent. *Answer:* 2.4 fluid ounces.

keyboard	display
Enter "C" . 0 5	0.05
× × 5	0.05

EXAMPLE 8-4: Estimate the blood alcohol concentration of a 165-pound person who has consumed 6 fluid ounces of 86-proof liquor in one hour. *Answer:* 0.12 percent.

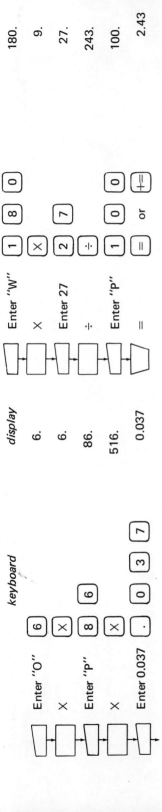

keyboard	display
Enter "O" 6	6.
×	6.
Enter "p" 8 6	86.
×	516.
Enter 0.037 . 0 3 7	0.037

(second flowchart, at right)

keyboard	display
Enter "W" 1 8 0	180.
×	9.
Enter 27 2 7	27.
÷	243.
Enter "p" 1 0	100.
= or +=	2.43

Electronic Calendar

Your electronic calculator can *compute* the day of the week of any date between January 1, 1900 and December 31, 1999. The interesting procedure outlined here shows you how. It looks a bit complex at first glance, but it actually is quite simple. There are three formulas:

$$A = (\text{Month} - 1) \times 30 + \text{Day} + \text{Correction}$$
$$B = \text{Year} \times 365.25 \quad \textit{Truncate Answer}$$
$$C = \frac{A + B}{7}$$

EXAMPLE 8-6: What day of the week is July 4, 1976? You begin the procedure by expressing the date of interest in numerical form. July 4, 1976 becomes 7/4/76, where "Month" = 7, "Day" = 4, and "Year" = 76.

Next, examine "Year" to determine if it is a leap year. If you aren't sure, simply divide the number by 4. If the answer is a whole number (no fractional part), then "Year" is a leap year. There is one exception: 1900 was *not* a leap year.

Now, look up the appropriate correction factor in the table below. In our example, 1976 is a leap year, and the correction factor for July is 1.

Correction Factor Table

	Jan	Feb	Mar	Apr	May	June	July	Aug	Sept	Oct	Nov	Dec
Reg. Year	0	1	-1	0	0	1	1	2	3	3	4	4
Leap Year	-1	0	-1	0	0	1	1	2	3	3	4	4

The algorithm below details the arithmetic calculations. We'll describe the procedure here.

The first step is to solve the first formula. "A" turns out to be 185.

Next, solve the second equation and truncate the answer (discard all digits to the right of the decimal point). Hence, B equals 27759 (in this example there are no digits to be discarded by truncation).

The third step is to plug "A" and "B" into the third formula. This yields a value for "C" of 3992.

In this specific example, "C" is an integer. Most of the time, "C" will have a fractional part. Examine "C" carefully and ignore all digits except the first two digits *to the right* of the decimal point. For our example, the digits are 00.

Finally, consult the following table to determine the day of the week.

Digits	Day of Week
00	Sunday
14	Monday
28	Tuesday
42	Wednesday
57	Thursday
71	Friday
85	Saturday

Thus, July 4, 1976 falls on a Sunday.

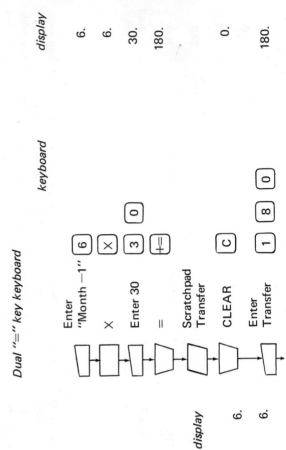

	keyboard	display
Enter "A"	[1] [8] [5]	185.
+	[+]	185.
Enter "B"	[2] [7] [7] [5] [9]	27759.
÷	[÷]	27944.
Enter 7	[7]	7.
=	[=]	3992.

Single "=" key keyboard

	keyboard	display
Enter "Month −1"	[6]	6.
×	[×]	6.

Dual "=" key keyboard

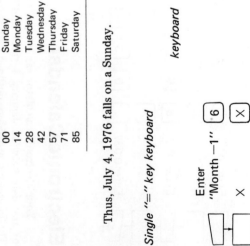

	keyboard	display
Enter "Month −1"	[6]	6.
×	[×]	6.
Enter 30	[3] [0]	30.
=	[±=]	180.
Scratchpad Transfer		
CLEAR	[C]	0.
Enter Transfer	[1] [8] [0]	180.

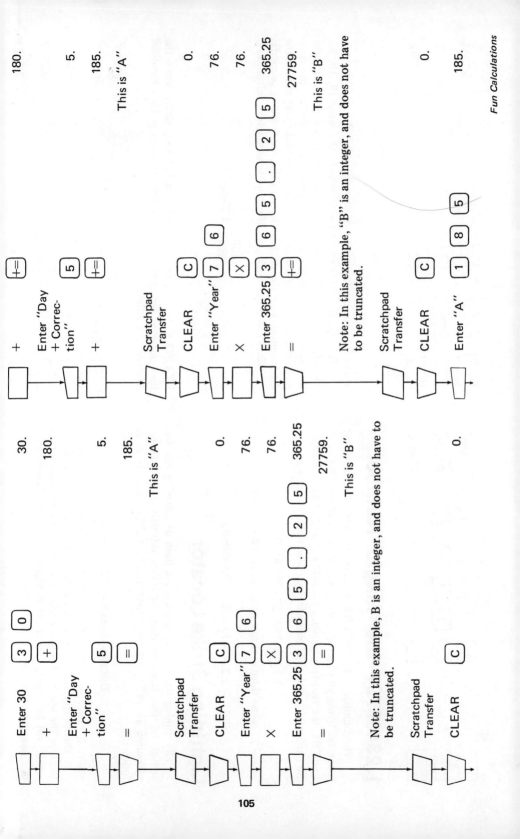

Fun Calculations

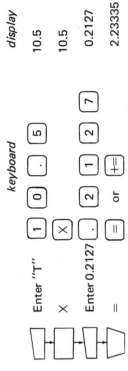

	display
÷	27944.
Enter 7	7.
=	3992.

	display
+	185.
Enter "B"	27759.
+	27944.

1.2345679—the "Magic" Number

The number 1.2345679 has an amazing, and quite unusual, property. When you multiply it by any multiple of nine between 9 and 81, the resulting product consists entirely of a single digit, the particular multiple of nine that you selected! For example,

$$1.2345679 \times 27 = 33.333333$$

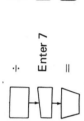

where 27 is the third multiple of nine (27 = 3 × 9), and

$$1.2345679 \times 81 = 99.999999$$

where 81 is the ninth multiple of nine (81 = 9 × 9).

Try out the other multiples of nine in the series (9, 18, 36, 45, 54, 63, and 72) to prove the point. Actually, this computation can be very useful. It is a fast way to "exercise" the complete display capabilities of a calculator to make sure that all the digits, along with the arithmetic circuitry, are working properly.

Here's another intriguing, if not quite as magical, calculation:

$$\frac{400}{324} = 1.2345679$$

Lightning Strike Locator

By timing the interval between a flash of lightning and the arrival of the thunder clap, you can estimate the distance, measured in *miles*, to the strike location. The formula is as follows:

$$\text{Distance (in miles)} = T \times 0.2127$$

where T = time between flash and thunder (in seconds).

This procedure assumes an ambient air temperature of 65°F. Because the speed of sound in air varies with air temperature, the result will be slightly incorrect at higher or lower temperatures. For maximum accuracy, use a stopwatch to measure the time interval.

EXAMPLE 8-7: How far away is a lightning strike when the time interval between flash and thunder clap is 10.5 seconds? *Answer:* 2.2 miles.

	keyboard	display
Enter "T"	1 0 . 5	10.5
×	×	10.5
Enter 0.2127	. 2 1 2 7	0.2127
=	= or +=	2.23335